THE CHURCH
THAT WENT
UNDER

St Nicholas, Sevenoaks

THE CHURCH THAT WENT UNDER

A building project that seemed impossible

Julia E M Cameron

Paternoster Press
Boswell Books

First published in 1999 by Paternoster Press in association with Boswell Books

Paternoster Press is an imprint of Paternoster Publishing, PO Box 300, Carlisle, Cumbria, CA3 0QS, UK *www.paternoster-publishing.com*

Boswell Books is based on St Nicholas Church, Sevenoaks, Kent TN13 1JA, UK
www.stnics.clara.net

Scripture quotations are taken from the Holy Bible: New International Version © 1973, 1978, 1984 by the International Bible Society. Published in Great Britain by Hodder and Stoughton Ltd.

British Library Cataloguing in Publication Data
Cameron, Julia Evelyn Mure
The Church that went under: A building project that seemed impossible
St Nicholas Church (Sevenoaks, England)
1. Church buildings – England – Sevenoaks
I. Title
283.4 ' 2236
ISBN 0-85364-937-5

Front cover photo: Mark Davey (*Sevenoaks Chronicle*).
Back cover tapestry deer used with permission, from *The New Church Kneeler Book* by Angela Dewar (Search Press).
Cover design: Chris Gander Design Associates, Croydon, UK.

Printed in Singapore by Star Standard Industries (Pte)

For Dinah, Daniel, Dodie and Boaz

Come and see St Nick's some time!

Acknowledgements

I arrived in Sevenoaks only a few months before St Nicholas went 'into exile' and James Longley took over the church building. This meant I was dependent on people who have lived here much longer than I for their stories and their reflections. My grateful thanks go to everyone who has given time to talk with me in my home or theirs, or on the telephone, or in church.

It was Miles and Sara Thomson's idea that this book be written, to tell not of an architectural feat – though it is unique in the world, so far as we know - but rather of how God moved in people's lives to bring about the events. Their help was invaluable.

Eve Wilmot generously lent me her late husband's papers; Paul and Janet Batchelor took me through the interface of faith and finance; Brigadier Ian Dobbie recalled for me his days as Project Director; Doris Colgate, Joan Banks, Cyril Best and David and Margaret Killingray filled the gaps in my local history; Tony Jennings and Mike Talbot reconstructed their time as churchwardens through the critical years; and Terry Boxall walked me through his liaison role as the church prepared to move back 'home'. I could not have done without any of them.

My thanks go also to Jean Watson for her editorial comments; to Adrienne Thompson for proof-reading the script; to Tom and Rachel McHugh for their map and diagrams; to Alex Watson and Mark Davey (both of the *Sevenoaks Chronicle*) and to Marilynn Sowerby, Barbara Lloyd, Peter Stewart, Stuart Ross, Mark Ellis and Wendy Billington for their photographs; and to Paul Dunn for managing the local sales.

The design and production team made the whole process easy. I commend Chris Gander of Design Associates, Croydon, and Michele Loke and Lee Sook Hian of Star Standard Industries, Singapore, for creating the book you are holding; and Mark Finnie, Nancy Lush and Ruth McBrien at Paternoster Press for making possible the distribution channels we had been hoping for.

In short, I have received contributions and expert advice in a wide range of ways. Where I got things right, it was thanks to you. Where I got things wrong, it was my fault entirely.

Contents

Foreword

St Nicholas Church, Sevenoaks, will always have a special place in my affections. After graduating and then completing my teacher training, I arrived in the town in 1971 to take up my first teaching post at Sevenoaks School. When I entered St Nicholas I knew nobody, but by the end of that day I had had lunch with the churchwarden and his wife (Mr and Mrs Claude Finney) and had been taken up the tower! Within a very short space of time I was helping to lead the youth work, and serving on the Parochial Church Council. I became a Reader, and helped in the first Family services. It was through my involvement with St Nicholas that I began to sense God was calling me to be ordained.

Through the Volunteer Service Unit at Sevenoaks School and the town's Volunteer Bureau, I recognised the importance of getting involved in the community. I came to see that the mission of the Church lay in building as many bridges as possible between itself and the community. From all I have heard about the undercroft, I believe it will help tremendously in this. I remember clearly how we felt the lack of anywhere to gather socially after services. It was important to have somewhere, so that friendships could deepen and those on the fringe could get to know members of the church.

It is now nearly 20 years since St Nicholas sent me, with my wife, Sarah, on the path to ordination. We have served the Lord in the four corners of the country. I have found few churches where so many people have been formed and shaped by the gospel for positions of leadership - in society at large, and in the Church, both as lay and ordained ministers.

The Bible makes clear that there are no prizes for having so many gifts – only responsibilities. I thank God for what I personally gained and learned from his people at St Nicholas. I pray this book may add momentum to the coming of his kingdom.

James Jones *Bishop of Liverpool*
April 1999

Easter Sunday morning. The banners read 'Christ is risen'.

Chapter 1

A medieval building for the 21st century *or* 'If I was going there, I wouldn't start from here'

Some visitors on holiday in County Cork asked a local farmer for directions. Hearing where they wanted to get to, he replied, 'If I was going there, I wouldn't start from here.' It may not have been the most helpful advice, but it summed up their plight in a moment. There is a sense in which the parish church of St Nicholas, Sevenoaks, found itself in a similar predicament. It was built for medieval England. To transform this ancient building into one which meets 21st century needs would be no simple task. It would have been a lot easier to design something new. But that was not an option. Its members, like the hapless holidaymakers, *had* to start from where they were.

The story of this church's transformation covers 30 years, and hopes were raised and dashed many times over that period.

St Nicholas has a long history. Some local historians date its earliest part as far back as AD 950, and evidence of a Saxon building was found during the archaeological excavations which preceded the construction of the undercroft. Together with the symbol of the seven acorns representing the famous seven oak trees, St Nicholas has been almost synonymous with the name of the town itself for over a thousand years. Travellers used its grounds as a safe place to camp overnight, while travelling down the old road to Rye, superseded now by the A21, a mile to the west. And over the centuries since, townspeople have doubtless sought comfort from its presence, if not within its walls, as they prayed for God's protection from the Black Death and the Plague, and as they remembered their fathers, sons and brothers in the two world wars.

The church stands at the far southern end of the High Street, almost opposite Sevenoaks School, which was founded in the reign of Elizabeth I. It is surrounded by a typical town graveyard, and the headstones tell the stories of Sennockian families over hundreds of years.[1] The road through the town goes into a bottleneck double bend not far from the church, and when it is busy, a driver's attention is focused on steering the car between the oncoming traffic and the narrow nearside pavement. This part of the town was designed for the 13th century! But then the road opens out, and the church comes into view all of a sudden, bringing the Anglo-Saxons, Elizabethans, Jacobeans, Victorians and Edwardians all into the context of time, and of eternity. It has served every age as a place of Christian worship. Whether one believes anything, or nothing at all, a medieval building like this is a fine sight. It is not surprising that the people of Sevenoaks wanted to preserve it as that.

In this book you will read a remarkable story. Visitors to the town who recall driving through that bottleneck bend a few years ago, and coming upon the church on the right hand side, could drive past now, and be forgiven for thinking nothing has changed. Such was the genius of the way the new facilities have been designed, for they are underground.

Everyone knew that to build underground would cost money, a great deal of money – well over £2,000,000. Church members also knew that there were no massive trusts to draw from. There was a Parish Hall, half a mile away, which could be sold, but even that would raise only a small proportion of what was needed. And the early 1990s was not an easy time financially. The phrase 'negative equity' suddenly appeared, and its reality became a serious issue for house owners caught in its trap. For those who did have capital, interest rates dropped. The boom of the 1980s was over.

This was the context in which it became clear that St Nicholas Church badly needed more space. Previous rectors had worked extremely hard to have earlier plans for an extension accepted, but for one reason or another, they had come to nothing. Then Miles Thomson arrived as the 51st Rector of Sevenoaks in 1987, and was given a special remit to sort out the accommodation needs. Within a few years, a suitable scheme had been devised, but it was dauntingly ambitious and expensive. Would it be accepted in the difficult economic climate? And even if it was, how would the money be raised? The money was raised, and in 1995 a unique and distinctive feature was added to the most ancient building in the town.

I recount these events for three reasons. *First* so the people of

Sevenoaks who love their town, and who love the landmark of St Nicholas, can read the inside story. *Secondly* so that members of the church family, many of whom have arrived since the building work was completed, can be filled in on what happened. *Thirdly* for the sake of churches up and down the country who are finding their own buildings inadequate, to show what can be done.

This is not a 'success story' in the sense of moving from one easy goal to the next, and on to win the cup. Over a period of 30 years there were all sorts of setbacks, as plans were proposed, then rejected. Those closely involved have vivid memories of times when it seemed plain that God was on their side, and of times when the biggest impact seemed to come from those who wanted the whole project forgotten. But they pressed on. An all-but-impossible sum would be needed in gifts, made willingly, from one parish church. That alone must have made the whole venture seem very unlikely to succeed.

Was this a special work of God, right here in southeast England? Sevenoaks residents must make up their own minds. The members of St Nicholas believe it was.

The Afterword by John Stott grounds the life of the church today in the teaching of the early church. Using the pattern of church life and church growth in the first century, he applies it to our post-secular, post-Christian, postmodern 21st century.

Chapter 2

This is Sevenoaks

Sevenoaks is widely known as a pleasant, even enviable, place to live, and it has drawn the attention of writers and poets, painters and historians.

The parkland around Knole House, open to the public by the kindness of Lord Sackville, is barely three minutes' walk from the High Street, and it stretches out across a thousand acres, as home to some six hundred deer.[1] Its paths are well known and well used by people from the surrounding area, as well as from Sevenoaks itself, and many offer commanding views of St Nicholas. Knole Park still bears the marks of the hurricane which opened up these vistas, and so famously uprooted six of the town's more recent 'seven oaks'. Tree trunks of massive girth lie around to tell the story of how they were ripped effortlessly from the ground on that fearful night of 16 October 1987.

The Pleasant Town of Sevenoaks by Sir John Dunlop, which has become the received work on the town's history, closes with a passionate plea to future town planners.[2] The author was aware that the town's location could be very attractive for future development: 'poised between the great city and the open countryside, lying slightly to one side of the main axis between Britain and Continental Europe'. It had the potential to grow in 'increasing charm, culture and beauty' but could also fall prey to pragmatic speculators. These were shrewd observations. The book was written in Dunlop's retirement, and he died in 1974. His closing plea was this:

> May the hope be here expressed that whatsoever new and architecturally brilliant buildings may arise, they will never be allowed to over-top the grey tower of St Nicholas on the hill, the foundation stone of historic Sevenoaks.

Dunlop's wish has stuck in people's minds, and struck a chord. As long as local town planners comply with that restraint, the constancy of the skyline will act as an eloquent tribute to him.

Some tall new office blocks had sprung up in the late 1960s, in the

lower part of Sevenoaks. These probably gave rise to his need for caution.
They were not architecturally brilliant and parts were to remain
unoccupied for several years in the recession. So to date, that 90-foot
church tower retains its position as the highest point.

Commuting – a way of life

Sevenoaks is on the main rail line between London Charing Cross and
Dover. Half an hour by train from Charing Cross, and less than that from
Cannon Street and London Bridge stations, it is one of the obvious choices
of town for commuters to live. The modest station, with just four platforms,
records over three million 'station uses' per year, with an estimated annual
rise of seven per cent per annum.[3] The rush hour is under way by
06.10am, and the 06.58am fast train offers standing room only by the time
it reaches Sevenoaks.

The stream of human traffic continues down the staircase to
Platform 1 for well over two hours. The reverse process starts soon after
5.00pm but many are still pouring out of trains very much later. Bankers,
lawyers, engineers, university lecturers, accountants, journalists, secretaries,
fashion designers. The columns of people moving fast and purposefully to
and from the car parks, and along the roads leading to the station, come in
bursts as trains for the capital leave or draw in. The line of taxis and cars
dropping off and picking up commuters morning and evening inches in
and out of the car park, circling its narrow island. A friendly urban fox with
a lean and hungry look has become a familiar sight, and manages to win
the goodwill of taxi drivers grabbing a sandwich or some fish and chips.

But despite the numbers who commute to work, this is not a
'dormitory town'. It has a life and identity of its own, and one detects a
certain pride in it, even from those who spend almost all their weekday
waking hours elsewhere.

Schools

Sevenoaks has a typical mix of state and private education at primary and
secondary levels. Sevenoaks School is one of the oldest schools in England,
with 950 pupils, more than a third of whom are boarders, many from
overseas. Walthamstow Hall draws 450 junior and senior girls, and has a

small boarding house. Combe Bank School, in the village of Sundridge, is an independent girls' day school with pupils from five to 18. Wildernesse Boys' School and Bradbourne School for Girls, both situated at the northern end of the town, are Grant Maintained secondary schools – each with over 500 pupils.

There are two schools for children with special needs. Dorton House School caters superbly for blind and visually-impaired children, on a beautiful campus in the adjacent village of Seal; it has just over 100 pupils up to age of 16, half of whom board. The former West Heath School, a little over a mile from the church, closed in 1998, and has now reopened as The New School at West Heath, a privately run centre for severely ill or abused children.

Hundreds of secondary school pupils take the train or cram into buses for Orpington, Tonbridge and Tunbridge Wells where schools compete for places in the coveted first column of the national league tables. St Nicholas fosters links with these more distant schools as well as with local ones, as many members of its youth groups – Centrepoint, Campaigners and Contact – travel out of town from Monday to Friday.

Through staff, governors and pupils who are members of the church, there are links with all the town's primary schools.[4] But its closest link is with its own Church School, Lady Boswell's, which dates back to 1675. The Rector is ex-officio a Foundation Governor, and the St Nicholas Parochial Church Council (PCC)[5] appoints three other members of its governing body. In reality a much greater proportion of the governors are active members of the church.

'Lady B's' is widely recognised as a successful school and every year the Reception class is over-subscribed. Daphne Harrison, Chairman of the Governors, explains, 'The whole governing body shares the head's determination to maintain a Christian ethos in every aspect of school life. This is vitally supported by a group of parents who meet weekly in school to pray. What is wonderful is that the foundations of its success are attributed by everyone to its strong Christian values. And that includes parents and OFSTED inspectors who themselves make no Christian profession.'

One public expression of the partnership between the church and the school is the school's anniversary service held in St Nicholas. This gives an opportunity for the whole church family to pray together for the life of the school, and to see the pupils in action. The school orchestra provides the music, the children sing something they have learned in their morning assembly, and teachers read the Bible lesson and lead in prayer.

The church in the town

St Nicholas draws together people who spend their weekdays in all sorts of ways. There are those who stand on Platform 1 for their morning train, along with hundreds of others, hopeful of a seat as far as London Bridge or Charing Cross before strap-hanging on the Underground. There are others who walk or drive to work locally – schoolteachers, office workers, shopkeepers, cleaners, doctors. Then there are housewives, retired people, and those between jobs, who can spend more time in their immediate neighbourhood. You could call this St Nicholas 'at large'. Or, better still, a small part of the worldwide body of Christ, bringing his presence to bear on the nitty-gritty of day-to-day life in southeast England.

St Nick's, as the church is affectionately known, has formal links with the town on several levels. As well as being a Foundation Governor at Lady Boswell's, Miles Thomson is chaplain to the girls at Combe Bank. He is also chaplain to the scouts, and its annual St George's Day Parade finishes with a gathering in the church. The town's civic service takes place in St Nicholas annually, when the newly-elected mayor is about to take office. A special invitation is sent to all Councillors, and the service includes prayer for them in their roles in local government. And as chaplain to the local branch of the Royal Naval Association and Royal British Legion, and Rector of the parish church, Miles leads the town's Remembrance Day service at the war memorial on The Vine.

But the informal linking of church members through their employment and their friendships is the widest-spread presence of the life of St Nicholas in the life of the town.

Town life

Sevenoaks is a favoured town, and its leafy roads show the care of its local council and community over decades. But like any other town in Britain, it has its share of domestic strife, of poverty on estates owned by housing associations, of single parenthood, of unemployment, of loneliness.

Several charities have opened second-hand clothes shops over the past few years, and some stretch to books and bric-a-brac as well. Quality of merchandise is often very high, and for many residents a glance in them is part of the High Street shopping routine. The Sevenoaks Volunteer Bureau was founded in 1972 and has some 250 volunteers on its books at any given time, lending help either to individuals or to local charities.

The main weekly market is held on Wednesdays. A much smaller group of stalls selling a variety of wares – fruit and vegetables, clothes, fish, flowers, and local art - cluster at the top of the High Street on Saturdays. Sevenoaks has held a general market since the thirteenth century, and had a livestock market as far back as the late eighth century, according to some local sources. These markets became part of its culture.

There is very little local manufacturing now. Marley Tiles had a factory in Dunton Green, Sevenoaks, until the mid 1990s when the site was redeveloped as a giant Tesco store. At the same time, Hodder and Stoughton's main offices, then also in Dunton Green, moved into larger premises in Euston Road, north London, when the business was sold to the Headline group and became Hodder Headline. The Vestry Estate, beyond the well-established Sainsbury's Superstore, is now largely made up of light industry and new car sales. The famous A-Z Map Company Ltd, founded by Phyllis Pearsall in 1936, moved to the Vestry Estate in 1962, but outgrew these units by the early 1990s. Its next move was to a 'brown field site' in Borough Green, seven miles east, where the new head office was opened in 1993. The redoubtable Mrs Pearsall's motto, for herself and for her team, was 'On we go!' and that remains the watchword for the hundred or so staff working for the company now.[6]

The *Sevenoaks Chronicle* was founded in 1881 as an amalgam of three other newspapers. It was a timely start for a new paper. The opening of the railway line to London in the 1860s had brought a steady rise in population, and the Education Acts of the 1870s had helped increase literacy. It was the *Chronicle* which announced to the town the arrival of the earliest telephone in a Sevenoaks home, and of the first car. The paper passed into new ownership in 1897, by which time it was already gaining a reputation for its independent voice. Indeed in January 1900 it noted in its editorial: 'Some of our councillors are morbidly sensitive to criticism'. It was then being printed by J Salmon, whose name was to become one of the best known in British printing.

The *Chronicle* is now published each Thursday in two editions: the main edition, serving the town itself and its western villages, and the Borough Green edition, serving the eastern area. Its circulation is around 14,500 with an estimated readership of nearly half the area's residents.

The other famous landmark

The Vine Cricket Ground, at the north end of the High Street, shaded by the new line of 'seven oaks', is world famous among cricket lovers. Like the church, the cricket ground is known to everyone in the area. The cricket club has some 150 playing members, but many others use its facilities, as the cricket pavilion is also a venue for a range of non-sporting functions.

The ground, which had once been part of the Knole Estate, was presented to the town by the third Duke of Dorset in 1773 'to be a cricket ground forever'. No one knows when cricket was first played there, but the earliest reported match took place on the 6 September 1734 when Lord John Philip Sackville led the Gentlemen of Kent against the Gentlemen of Sussex, pitting 'his team and his purse'. In 1769 it was to make history, when one J Minshall, playing for Sussex, scored the first ever century in the sport.

This is Sevenoaks: outside and inside

This, then, is Sevenoaks at the turn of another century. A town which is outwardly comfortable, but where some families genuinely struggle financially. A town whose commuters stride purposefully to the station in the mornings, some carrying a high level of responsibility, and of stress. A town with a cinema, a theatre, a library, a swimming pool, and an ever-growing number of pubs and restaurants. A town with a population of 18,000 who, in common with human beings across the globe and throughout history, have more needs than just food and shelter.

In his book *The Contemporary Christian*, John Stott speaks of 'a universal, threefold human aspiration'.[7] Drawing from a wide range of 20th century thinkers and writers, including Mother Teresa, Woody Allen, Bertrand Russell, and columnists from *The Independent* and *The Economist*, he explains this in terms of 'the quest for transcendence', 'the quest for significance', and 'the quest for community'. Like others around the world, many Sevenoaks residents sense a transcendent presence outside the created universe; in a fast-changing, computerised society, they feel a need to matter; and in a world where little value is placed on family units, they need to know they belong.

If the first century Christian gospel is to relate to 21st century society, the Church must engage with people in meeting all these needs.

Chapter 3

Problems and a solution

Before coming to St Nicholas in 1987 to succeed Canon Kenneth Prior, Miles had spent 13 years in Harold Wood, Essex, as vicar of St Peter's, a church of similar size. With all the expected jibes from family and friends, he was formally instituted as Rector on April Fools' Day.

Over the previous decade and more, many churches up and down the country had begun to take stock of their buildings and ask new questions about their suitability. St Nicholas was just one of these. For years, there had been real concern over the inadequacy of accommodation on site. Under the leadership of Eric McLellan in the 1960s, and then again under Kenneth Prior in the 1970s and early 1980s, much effort had been expended in trying to find a solution. The PCC urged that this matter should be an early priority for Miles.

Gaining permission is not easy

Householders can have all sorts of stories to tell of their frustration in trying to build an extension, or to change the use of their home to incorporate a small business. The fact that a word like 'bureaucracy' should enter the language tells its own story, though most would concede that the hoops which planning departments put people through are genuinely helpful in steering – or staying – the course of development in residential and in business areas. But for all the difficulties a home-owner may encounter, the matter is much more complex for a church. And the more so if it is in a conservation area.

Church buildings do not belong to the congregation, nor does the PCC have jurisdiction over them, though it is bound to keep them in good order. Permission to alter a church building can be given only by the Chancellor of the

church buildings do not belong to the congregation

21

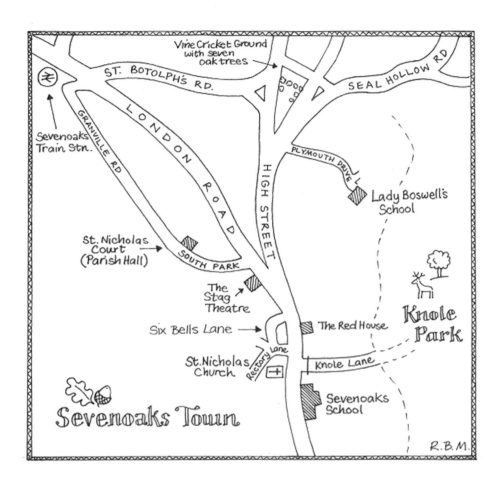

diocese, on behalf of the Bishop. The Chancellor himself is a layman, usually a former lawyer or judge. Outside courts have had this kind of jurisdiction over church buildings and their burial grounds for several hundred years.

But even that is not the whole story. Some 25 million people in the UK describe themselves as 'Church of England', perhaps because they were christened or married in their parish church, or simply because they are not anything else. And of that number, those with concerns about local plans feel their voice should be heard. It was hardly surprising for there to be a reaction from Sevenoaks residents to proposed structural change at St Nicholas, for though they may not worship there, the Anglicans still felt it to be 'their church'.

The need for more space had been a pressing one for twenty years. By 1987 it was acute. Previous plans for an extension had been vetoed, but the matter could not rest. God was at work in people's lives, drawing them to church in numbers. St Nick's had a responsibility to act, and must not shirk it. The financial hurdle, however, would be huge, and some felt their faith faltering at the sheer magnitude of the costs.

Secretary of State intervenes

In October 1981 and in December 1982, the church had approached Sevenoaks District Council with proposals for an extension. In each case, care was taken in the design. It needed to fit in sympathetically with the building's medieval foundation, and its 19th and 20th century additions. Following both occasions, the correspondence columns of the *Sevenoaks Chronicle* carried angry opposition. Those living nearby naturally wanted to guard against increase in traffic and noise, and had a special interest in maintaining the architectural integrity of the building. Here was an ancient, attractive church, loved by its members as much as by anyone else, and no one with any aesthetic sensibility wanted to see a 'carbuncle' added to it.

The *first* proposal was for an octagonal building, which would be reached through a covered walkway, largely out of sight from the main road. It would have cost £100,000. This was accepted by the Town Council, but pressure from the Sevenoaks Society and the Royal Fine Arts

Early evening light catches the blossom and the headstones. No-one wanted to see a 'carbuncle'
added to this ancient, attractive building

Commission drew it to the attention of Michael Heseltine, then Secretary of State for the Environment. He called in the plans for an enquiry. It would have been expensive to pursue the matter, and it seemed unlikely that permission would be granted, given local feeling. Weighing things carefully, the PCC decided to withdraw their proposal.

The *second* plan was for an extension against the north wall of the church, between the protruding vestry and the north door (both 20th century additions). This was received as a much better solution, and judged by Councillor John Buckwell, a member of St Nicholas, and later Mayor of Sevenoaks, as 'a triumph of compromise'. Spirits rose. A happy way forward had been found, or so it was thought. But again the Sevenoaks Society expressed concern. This plan would require the removal

a truer perspective on those difficult years became possible

of a 15th century wall, and, as the extension adjoined the recent additions, would 'draw attention to less-interesting parts of the building'. Once more feelings ran high, and yet again Mr Heseltine intervened. For a second time the PCC deemed it wise to withdraw. There must have been a massive surge of discouragement, but this could not be allowed to dash hopes for the future, nor to cause a rift between the church and the town.

Surely there was a way ahead which would not alienate local residents - a solution which would commend the gospel, and not raise antagonism against the church leaders.

When that way forward was found, a truer perspective on those difficult years became possible. Neither of these plans would have given the amount of space needed for the future. For all the time and energy spent, and for all the disappointment, it was clear in retrospect that Mr Heseltine's intervention was providential. The words 'but God' sum up much of what was to happen over the next few years, as he worked to change situations, and to change people's minds, in answer to prayer. The Sevenoaks Society, the Royal Fine Arts Commission and the Department for the Environment might appear to have overruled the PCC's plans in the interests of the publics they each served. Perhaps the higher truth was simply: 'But God meant it for good'.

Children's work on Sundays

When Miles and his wife, Sara, arrived in Sevenoaks, the children's and young people's groups had developed to such a wonderful extent that the leaders who had built them up could be described as victims of their own success. They had worked hard, and their welcoming attitude and imaginative teaching resulted in there being some 280 on the roll. Junior Worship, as the three-12s group was then called, met in Lady Boswell's School, nearly a mile away from St Nicholas. Centrepoint (early teens) met in the Parish Hall, half a mile away. The crèche squeezed into the church office, built on the side of the Rectory.

For parents with children spanning two or even all three age groups, it was an achievement just to deliver them all on time to the right place, and then to get to the morning service themselves. Collecting the family afterwards meant parents had no opportunity to talk with anyone, as they had to leave promptly for the reverse operation. The Monday to Friday 'school run' was now the 'Sunday school run' and almost as pressured. There was an obvious need to bring the whole operation together, and not have it strewn around the town. And this was for more than practical reasons. The church members were not able to get to know each other, simply because of logistics. If a church is to be part of 'Christ's body' in a town, the spiritual dimensions of these kinds of difficulties have to be looked at seriously. As so often in life, spiritual and practical considerations run in parallel; and the spiritual solution proves to be the practical one.

There was space for only 65 cars near the church, but this meant parking bumper to bumper, and defying all rules of safety, or of access for the emergency services. After dropping off their children, parents could rarely find car parking spaces, and this was no incentive for them to come to church. In fact it was a silent encouragement for them simply to take the children to their groups, go home, and then collect them afterwards.

It is well known that a large proportion of Christians are converted when they are young, through the influence of Christian friends at school,

The Batchelors' story

Paul and Janet Batchelor met when they were at Cambridge, and married in 1969. Both had gone to their local village churches as children and, as undergraduates, had enjoyed the sermons at Great St Mary's, the university church. But after leaving university their church interest waned and their Christian faith was neglected. 'We had been churchgoers, but perhaps not real Christians,' they now acknowledge.

The Batchelors spent their first six years of married life in Africa, first in Swaziland then in Malawi. Paul, an economist, was working as a development planner for the governments there. They moved to Sevenoaks in 1975 and Paul, then a management consultant for Coopers & Lybrand, joined the commuters on Platform 1 when he was not travelling abroad. Once their two children, Emma and Jonathan, were old enough, Janet started to teach geography in local schools on a part-time basis.

Wanting their children to learn about the Bible, Paul and Janet took them to the monthly St Nicholas Family Services. Soon afterwards, Emma and Jonathan joined the weekly children's groups. 'But like so many others, we found it difficult to cope with getting our children to the groups, and then getting ourselves to church. So we tended just to drop the children, then come home,' said Janet. 'But we did go all together to the monthly Family Services.'

'St Nick's children's groups were pivotal to the renewal of our faith,' Paul observes. 'As Emma and Jonathan grew up, they became very committed, and we too began to benefit more and more from the quality of Bible teaching St Nick's offers.'

Both Janet and Paul had serious doubts about the undercroft project. Having lived for years in Africa, they thought it seemed self-indulgent. Perhaps more money should go to mission work instead? Paul resolved to express his concerns to Miles Thomson, stressing the importance of considering all the viable options, including the 'do nothing' option. 'Unless you consider doing nothing, you never understand the full benefits or the costs of different alternatives,' he said.

About six months later, completely unexpectedly, the then building fund treasurer resigned, and Paul was asked to replace him. 'I had a crowded diary, and knew it could only bring more pressure. But after much discussion and prayer, Janet and I decided it was right for me to accept. For both of us, it proved a faith-building exercise, and we were privileged to be part of it.'

The Clarkes' story

Roger Clarke is an audit manager for Unilever, and Charmian a part-time history teacher. They moved to Sevenoaks from Bristol in 1986 when Roger was transferred to the company's London office. The Clarkes have three children, now grown up. Richard, the youngest, was just three years old when the family came. They had been members of St Mary's, Stoke Bishop, in Bristol, and made it an early priority to find a church in Sevenoaks when they arrived.

At that point, Junior Worship was still held in Lady Boswell's School. Each Sunday, Roger and Charmian left the children there, and drove up the High Street for the morning service, sometimes arriving on time, sometimes slightly late. At St Mary's they had gone to church *together* as a family. For the Clarkes, who wanted to nurture spiritual values in their children, this was important.

Having to rush back to Lady Boswell's after the service to collect the children meant there was not time to talk with people and get to know them. It came as no surprise to them to discover that many parents were simply dropping their children off at Junior Worship then going home. Roger and Charmian could not do this, as they wanted to worship with other Christians, and to grow in their own faith. They valued the teaching ministry at St Nick's but found it impossible to feel a part of the church, sliding in as they did at the start of the service, and leaving straight away at the end. 'It didn't seem the right way to conduct family life,' said Charmian, 'and rushing to the service was not the best way to prepare ourselves for Sunday worship.'

They felt they could not go on like that, and realised they would have to make a decision. In the end they resolved to go to a different local church, which had a good Sunday school for children up to 11, even though there would be another bridge to cross three or four years later. When the children got older, they naturally wanted their peers around them, and Bible teaching which related to life as teenagers. By then, the St Nicholas children's work was all at Sevenoaks School and whole families could come to church together, and sit together for the first part of the service.

'St Nick's has given all three of our children a wide range of valuable friendships,' said Roger. 'Through Centrepoint and Contact they've been helped to understand Christian teaching in a way which enables them to make a commitment to Christ for themselves.'

through reading the Bible themselves, or perhaps through a university mission. As people move out into their working lives and take on mortgages, spiritual matters are often sidelined. Now that there is no social pressure for parents who are not Christians to have a baby 'christened', the next big opportunity for them to be linked with a church is when their children reach Sunday school age. Despite the influence of secular thought and materialist values, most parents want their children to learn about God. They may express it very basically, as knowing stories about Jesus. And they may feel inadequate themselves as teachers, if their own grasp of the Bible is minimal. What they need is a church that will welcome them, and make them feel at home.

the Monday-Friday school run was now the Sunday school run

The arrangements at St Nicholas made this virtually impossible. Once parents had delivered their children, it was almost time for the service to start. With the church car park already full, they had to use the Stag Theatre car park and walk up from there. It isn't far, but it generally meant arriving late at the service. And arriving late makes people feel conspicuous.

After careful discussion with the churchwardens[1] and the PCC, Miles decided to tackle things in the short-term as soon as he could, and not wait for a long-term solution. By the autumn of 1987, all groups had moved up to meet in Sevenoaks School, opposite the church. The Headmaster generously made this provision without charge. This meant that for the time being, families could spend Sunday mornings in the same part of the town.

Crossing the children over the High Street was not easy, given the flow of traffic, sharp bends and the narrow pavements. A group of men took it in turns to don fluorescent jackets and to hold up the stream of cars. Crossing duties started before the service began as children deposited things in their classrooms before coming into church, then the mass exodus

The Parish Hall in South Park (now St Nicholas Court)

came 20 minutes later. The 'crossing team' was back on duty at the end of the service, until the last child had come back over the road. This arrangement was a significant move forward but by no means the whole solution. Mercifully there were no accidents.

An outside possibility

Miles had served his curacy at All Souls Church, Langham Place, in central London, a stone's throw from Oxford Circus, and just opposite the BBC. This city centre church was designed by the famous Regency architect, John Nash, who influenced so much of the nineteenth century grandeur of London's West End. Though All Souls and St Nicholas had nothing in common architecturally, there were inescapable parallels between the two. Both needed more space on site, and had problems finding it. All Souls is a church on a traffic island, so it could not 'throw out a wing' when it needed to expand, in the 1970s. Church leaders could see how spiritual growth was being hindered through simple lack of accommodation for training, for meetings, for fellowship.[2] In 1972, Robert Potter of the Sarum Partnership, an architect with a remarkable gift for re-designing churches, developed the Waldegrave Hall underneath All Souls. The Thomsons were in Harold Wood by the time this took place, but they kept close links with All Souls through the whole process of praying and planning. It was a massive undertaking, calling for truly sacrificial giving. With God's help, the money was raised. It was a miracle. Could God do it again, in Sevenoaks? And might a plan to dig *underneath* the church win sympathetic support? These were some of the questions in people's minds.

To contact Robert Potter, and to gain from his experience and wisdom, seemed the obvious step to take. He had brought his genius to Above Bar Church in Southampton's city centre, which was rebuilt to include shops at street level, and designed a basement for Lincoln College Library in Oxford, which involved going underneath an existing church. He had also been the surveyor for major structural work at both St Paul's Cathedral and Chichester Cathedral.[3] He understood ancient buildings and had a feel for modern ones. His wife, Margaret, brought a background in interior design. They were a team, and together they worked for God's glory. Robert Potter visited St Nick's that autumn, and with characteristic generosity, he prepared a drawing at no cost for the PCC to consider.

The ball was rolling again.

Chapter 4

Looking at the options

Suppose one of you wants to build a tower. Will he not first sit down and estimate the cost, to see if he has enough money to complete it? For if he lays the foundation and is not able to finish it, everyone who sees it will ridicule him, saying, 'This fellow began to build and was not able to finish.' (see Luke 14:25-35)

Jesus used a building project to help illustrate what it means to become a disciple. Just like people who are about to embark on a major construction, he said, anyone thinking hard about becoming a Christian also needs to count the cost. Jesus knew people's hearts. He knew that matters which touch our bank accounts are taken very seriously. And that is why he chose that illustration.

Whatever the way ahead for St Nick's, the monetary cost alone would be huge, and it had to be counted with care. For the church to look squarely at the options, someone would have to do a thorough feasibility study, weighing each one, and presenting the cold, hard data of what things meant in cash terms.

The man for the job

Tony Wilmot was a man of many parts. Miles and the churchwardens felt he would be an excellent choice for this, if he would take it on. For generations Tony's family had owned a paper mill in the village of Shoreham, six miles from Sevenoaks. He had been educated at Tonbridge School and, while still a pupil there, had joined the St Nicholas youth group, which met in the Parish Hall. That was in 1932. Though he spent most of his working life in West Africa, he always looked upon St Nicholas as his home church.

Tony died 18 months after the undercroft was opened. *The Times* and *The Daily Telegraph* both carried obituaries to him, noting his role in the undercroft, and the way his 'business acumen, permeated by his faith, drove the project through to completion.'[1] The experience he gained in his working life, and his love of St Nicholas, came together wonderfully.

The Times described his career as 'distinguished and wide-ranging' telling of how he entered the Colonial Service straight from university and, after the fall of Addis Ababa, became Secretary to the Government of British Somaliland at the age of 29. As Assistant District Commissioner in Northern Rhodesia (now Zambia) from 1938-1940, he developed such a facility in Chibemba that it was said his accent was indistinguishable from that of a native speaker. The obituary went on as follows:

> He was a man of great energy, and he would always look at things as they were, and then at what could be. That was evident on two levels: in the role he played in the political and economic development of West Africa, and in the way he identified potential in young people.

The Daily Telegraph writer picked up on a similar theme, and called him an 'influencer of influencers' noting:

> In all his activities he showed an unusual talent for spotting and helping young men who would rise to positions of power in future years. One such was Emeka Anyaoku, future secretary-general of the Commonwealth, whom he recruited as an undergraduate from Ibadan University.
>
> Wilmot was the moving spirit behind the formation of the Pan African Fellowship of Evangelical Students and used his extensive business travelling to help strengthen Christian Union groups in many universities.

He was indeed a man who would 'look at things as they were, and then at what could be'. Alongside this, he was blessed in good measure with that gift of dissatisfaction which, rightly handled, is essential for any Christian leader. Both papers picked up the story of how the Wilmots, in their retirement, worked to raise $200,000 to build a centre for postgraduate theological training in Nairobi, so African pastors could be trained in Africa. The land they found in Karen (named after Karen Blixen of *Out of Africa*) housed 'three chicken runs and a dogfood factory'. The wonderful incongruity of these being turned into a theological college has to raise a smile. It must have seemed the most unlikely scenario. Nairobi Evangelical Graduate School of Theology (NEGST) is now internationally recognised. It took more than the Wilmots' imagination to bring it into being. Here was another story which hinged on those two words: 'But God...'

The Wilmots had seen the unlikely happen; and their faith had been strengthened through it. As they reflected on the influence in the African Church of NEGST's two hundred or more graduates, they were continually reminded of the way God can work to achieve what seems impossible. It could not have been better preparation.

Realism

The very day after Tony and Eve Wilmot handed over their responsibility for NEGST in 1989, the telephone rang. It was Miles. Would Tony work on the feasibility study? Yes, he would. The dining room table of the Wilmots' home in Stone Street had been cleared of NEGST papers for only 24 hours; and now the wood was to be covered again solidly for the next six months.

Tony began work to find out all the available facts and their implications for all possible options. There was naturally a good deal of discussion around the church family about what should happen, but it was not all well-informed, partly because no one knew the answers to some things. The first recommendation Tony made, in the opening paragraph of his report, was that a day be set aside for prayer. He quoted Alfred Lord Tennyson in *Morte d'Arthur*: 'More things are wrought by prayer than this world dreams of '.

There were four main options: to do nothing; to explore once again an extension in the churchyard; to build in the Rectory grounds; to dig out an undercroft beneath the church.

Buildings and people

Tony's report looked first at a question in many people's minds: was it good to invest so much money in a building, for the sake of more space? He noted that the ministry of the Lord Jesus on earth began with an invitation to fishermen to become 'fishers of men' and ended with a much wider call. They were to 'go into all the world and preach the gospel', and for this they were promised the power of the Holy Spirit in their lives. So the Lord himself kept on diverting his listeners' attention from the here and now to the eternal. He did this in all sorts of places: in the open air, in private conversations in homes and at parties, and also in the synagogue, which was a magnificent building – expensive to construct and expensive to maintain.

Later, as Jewish attitudes to the gospel made it impossible to worship in the synagogue, the first Christians started meeting in homes. That practice has continued in countries where there are no churches or few churches because of the political regime, but it is not a practical solution. So though there are no specific guidelines in the Bible as to the kind of building to use, Christians are urged to meet *together*.

> '*more things are wrought by prayer than this world dreams of*'

The report then went on to cite examples of the kinds of difficulty the church was facing.

The facility of Sevenoaks School for the children's groups on a Sunday morning was marvellous, but there was no guarantee it would last indefinitely. And it was not ideal to be crossing children over a busy road each Sunday morning.

Contact, the youth group, drew up to a hundred older teens. Many were looking into the Christian faith and giving careful thought to its claims. This was a key ministry. It met on a Sunday evening in the Parish Hall, which was a bare and somewhat forbidding place, and difficult to heat in the winter. To ignore the needs of Contact would be regrettable, given the opportunities both to teach young Christians and to draw in their unbelieving friends. A number of Contact members came regularly to the evening service, and monopolised the pews in the south corner of the church. But it was felt that with integrated facilities, more would come to the service as well as to their own meeting afterwards. That has proved to be the case. On Sunday evenings now a good phalanx of Contact lay claim to certain rows of seats – still in the south corner. Tradition dies hard!

The Parish Hall was used for several midweek events, but its austerity and general lack of *ambience* held little attraction. Its position in town, several minutes' walk from the church, meant mothers and nannies who brought their children to the weekly 'Mum & Co' often failed to realise the group was attached to St Nicholas at all. This was no way to build bridges into church life.

The church office was too small to function as it needed to. As with any busy church, there were visits throughout the day from people making catering arrangements, delivering or collecting items, coming to see one of the clergy, using the photocopier, folding news sheets, or enquiring about marriage, baptisms or confirmation. The post of Rector's secretary is always held by a member of the church family, and that link with the life of St Nick's makes the office much more than an administrative centre. People are welcomed by name, and the place has a spiritual 'pulse'. In such cramped accommodation, even the most basic office function was under threat – it was difficult to file things in a way which made them easily retrievable. The ideal combination of efficiency, a friendly atmosphere, and space for people to sit down without interrupting the work of others, was no more than a dream.

Possible ways forward

In most church building projects, there is some opposition from the local community, and it can come in large part from those who do not go to church. There seems to be some kind of assumption that church buildings will look after themselves and continue to be maintained for the sake of offering visual pleasure to the public – even if their facilities are too outmoded to be useful.

There was general feeling in the town that the church should not be touched architecturally. This was not entirely logical, given the movement of history, and the fact that there had been significant changes to the structure on two occasions in the nineteenth century, when box pews and galleries had been removed, and again earlier in this century, when the vestry and north porch had been added. Most people seemed unaware of these changes. It was developments like those that enabled the site to continue as a meeting place for Christians.

It seemed that the church was in a cleft stick. Secular authorities seemed to assume that Christians would tend churches, and repair them when necessary. But they were oblivious to the fact that their restrictions could be making it impossible or impractical for a church family to remain in a building that was no longer suitable for its needs. St Nicholas' leaders and members had a love for their church, and were committed to its care. There could be no danger at all of an unseemly, unsightly addition.

Tony Wilmot described the need for development as 'a sensitive marriage between conservation and progress'. Future generations, he said, should not feel we had neglected or spoiled our heritage, but neither should they have to conclude that we had frozen progress. 'We have an overriding debt to our children and our children's children,' he wrote. 'Our future greatness lies with them and is to be promoted every bit as much as memorials of our past greatness.'

The 'do nothing' option may have won immediate support from the town, but it would simply have passed on problems to those who followed, and offered no solution to very real, pressing needs. It would have demanded no courage, and comparatively little money – only what would be needed for some necessary repairs to the Parish Hall and the church.

the 'do nothing' option would simply have passed on problems

The lowest-cost practical solution seemed to be a one-storey building in the southwest corner of the churchyard, linked to the church by a covered walkway, which could be partly sunk to ensure that the view of the tower was not impeded from any direction. However, this would mean reburying remains from graves in that area, and one of the strong objections to the 1982 plan had been the need for reburials. So such a plan would be unlikely to gain acceptance, especially as the church stands in a conservation area.

The third possibility was to build in the Rectory grounds. The downside of this was that the site would then not be fully integrated, even after a great deal of money had been spent and precious car-parking spaces had been lost. Planning permission was, anyway, unlikely, given the close proximity to the Rectory.

The fourth option was to dig the undercroft. It would be extremely expensive, but might win approval from the town. It would also free up the maximum parking space available on the parsonage land beside the Rectory. In the long-term, this looked like the best plan to adopt. However, it would mean spending a lot of money simply to explore its technical feasibility. Digging out halls beneath a medieval building had never been done before anywhere in the world. It was, as Robert Potter later described it, 'almost too challenging to do more than whisper'. Would church members have enough confidence in the PCC's judgment, and its sense of God's purpose, to give money for exploratory digs which, in the end, might show that an undercroft would not be possible? For a church to brace itself for large expenditure with a goal in sight is one thing; to give money when the goal is uncertain is another. Yet this intermediate sum would be necessary, in order to determine both the possibility of digging underneath, and what the final costs might be.

Tony Wilmot concluded his report by urging the PCC to forge ahead with the costs, and get to grips with whatever facts then became available. He wrote, 'My conviction is that we must make the choice on the basis of heaven's dividends, and then decide how to raise the capital.'

'We did it – you can too'

Michael Baughen, Bishop of Chester, had taken two churches through major building work. As a newly-ordained vicar he found himself in the vanguard of a major venture of faith at Holy Trinity, Platt Fields, in Manchester. Then he was appointed as Rector of All Souls, Langham Place, in London, at the critical stage prior to its major building project. He came down to St Nicholas one evening in September 1989 to exhort the church family, and to answer questions from his own experience.

Tony Wilmot had focused people's minds on 'heaven's dividends' and Michael Baughen endorsed that. 'Make sure you go for principles. If you need more space, to keep people on site after services so they can be made to feel properly welcomed, and brought into the church family, then go all out to achieve this. The money is a secondary matter.'

He spoke of what he had learned from the life of Moses when he arrived in Manchester. He had found himself asking the church family there, 'Do you actually believe in God?' If you believe that the God you worship is the same God who pulled back the waters of the Red Sea for the Israelites, surely he can handle the difficulties we face? He quoted the three stages of a process summed up by Hudson Taylor, the son of a Barnsley chemist who

make the choice on the basis of heaven's dividends

became a pioneer missionary to inland China. They were 'Impossible. Difficult. Done.' He added, 'This God can bring a building project through these stages. It *can* be done.'

Bishop Baughen had been close to several major projects in different parts of the country. None of them had been plain sailing, and he had witnessed despondency, even near despair at times. But in each of those churches in Manchester, Sheffield, Leicester, Reigate, Chislehurst and London, people had been changed as the projects had moved forward. They had learned more about God and more about prayer. Referring to the All Souls story, he said, 'We learned a lot about working with God through the project.' Then he drew on two remarkable stories to illustrate what he meant.

The first related to prayer. All site meetings at All Souls started with prayer. The workmen had felt uneasy about this in the first few weeks, and had perhaps been a little embarrassed. But they got used to it, and from time to time even asked the church to pray when they found something problematical. One afternoon the site manager asked for prayer as the local district inspector was being difficult. That evening, people prayed about the situation, not really knowing what to ask, but aware that this man was causing problems. The next morning, news came that he had been promoted. 'He was delighted and so were we,' commented Michael Baughen.

The second showed God's care and protection through one of the workmen. The telephone rang in the Rectory one evening at 10.30pm. It was the painter. He had just realised that he had left the electric water heater switched on at the top of the scaffolding. 'If it burns through, it'll set the place alight,' he said. Michael sped over to the church and found that the man had been right. Another half an hour, and the building would have gone up in flames.

One question which had arisen in every building project Michael had known was whether it was right for a church to spend so much on its own 'plant'. This question, he said, was raised by some with genuine concerns, and by others with a touch of disingenuity. If people preferred to make a substantial gift to overseas work instead, then they must feel free to do that. But it would not be right to think of the undercroft as 'spending money on ourselves'. It would be 'spending money for Christ's kingdom'. And as homes were becoming more and more comfortable, it was appropriate to think of *ambience* for a church, too, so when friends were invited to church, they would feel 'at home'. He added, 'In each of the projects I have seen, giving to a building project has released money to be given to other things, so the general giving in the church has gone up significantly.'

He urged the church to think of generations to come in Sevenoaks. 'It gives me joy,' he said, 'to see All Souls crowded, used and working, and to think of what it's done for hundreds and hundreds and *hundreds* of young people.'

Yes, it was a major project to embark on. Yes, it would mean serious financial sacrifice. But to work *with* God in this way would bring a new dimension to church life. 'Pray,' he said, 'that the spiritual will outmatch the material.' And he went on, 'There is a very major promise in Paul's letter to the Ephesians – that God is "able to do immeasurably more than all we can ask or imagine". Let's believe it!' That promise was to be turned back to over and over again.

Other interested parties

English Heritage and the Royal Fine Arts Commission both took a deep interest in the church plans on three counts. The building was medieval in origin; it formed a significant part of a conservation area; and its case had been highlighted in the early 1980s when Michael Heseltine had called in the earlier plans. Its raised position, on a ridge at the top of the town, made it a prominent feature from several vantage points. This was a wonderful site for a church building, but it just added to the weight of opposition against extensions in the churchyard.

At a town level, Tony Wilmot met with representatives of the Sevenoaks Society, the Friends of Sevenoaks Conservation group, and Sevenoaks District Council. These meetings all took time for careful preparation, but it was a good investment. In exploring the way ahead, there was every reason not to cause needless offence; every reason to let people know they had been heard and to work at accommodating them wherever possible.

conservation is intertwined with continued use and usefulness

If something had to be done, an undercroft was evidently the preference of the Sevenoaks Society. Friends of Sevenoaks Conservation preferred there to be no development of any sort at all. It was obviously not possible to gain their support, as something *had* to be done! Sevenoaks District Council recognised that conservation is intimately intertwined with continued use, and therefore with continued usefulness. Its Official Guide, which ran to 108 pages, with 25 illustrations including three churches, all outside the town boundary, made little mention of St Nicholas. The reference read simply:

> St Nicholas Church is also worth a visit. It dates back to 1122 and one of its rectors was John Donne, the metaphysical poet, in residence from 1616-1631.

It was only ever a Grade II listed building. In the circumstances, that fact and the somewhat dismissive reference in the Guide were definitely to be welcomed. The District Council was, however, reluctant to give its support while English Heritage still opposed the plans.

At the outset, English Heritage had said an undercroft would be unacceptable, and preferred a building on the car park, urging the District Council to vote against digging underneath. It was not until November 1991 that their permission was eventually given. This had taken 18 months of discussion, negotiation and compromise. And it was made clear that a keen interest would be taken in all external features including flights of steps, ramps and so forth.

'New money' for the right reasons

Robert Potter and Poul Beckmann of Ove Arup, specialist engineers, had begun to explore the possibilities of underpinning the church, and Tony Wilmot was in touch with archaeologists and with the Diocesan Chancellor about the graves beneath the floor. The undercroft was starting to look like a viable option from the engineering perspective. But one thing was without question in Tony's thinking, and in that of the Thomsons, the wardens and the PCC. If the idea was from God, the Holy Spirit would have to convince people not only of its possibility, but of its *desirability*. And the whole church membership, or the majority of its members, would need to want it sufficiently to put substantial financial backing into it.

From the beginning, the project had been called *Building for the Gospel* and the energy behind it had to be infused with a passion for the gospel, and a love of Christ. This need for extra room was to provide facilities for teaching, for training, for fellowship, for evangelism. It was not to make the church more comfortable or spacious as an end in itself. Here was a parish church set on a hill, known by everyone in the area, a building where Christians gathered to worship the living God together. The Church of England parish system could not be organised better in terms of influencing a country – there is a church building for every parish, and every home, shop, office, factory in the land is in one of those parishes. Money invested in this undercroft would bring benefit to the whole of the St Nicholas parish. And through the influence of its members, the benefits of that investment would extend much further.

from the beginning the project had been called 'Building for the Gospel'

Tony Wilmot was not only the driving force behind the building project. He was also Chairman of the missionary committee. This linking of responsibilities was a great advantage. Though Tony and Eve had spent many years in West Africa, and had a strong affinity with Africans, they were in every sense '*world Christians*'. Eve's grandfather, stroke of the Cambridge University boat, was one of the famous 'Cambridge Seven' – able young graduates who stunned the UK in 1885 by giving up the comfortable lives which they were guaranteed at home, and sailing for China as missionaries.[2] When people spoke of the financial needs and opportunities in world mission, they struck a chord in Tony's thinking; he was not unaware of them.

Tony's priorities were spiritual ones. He had exemplified that throughout his life. It has been said that more Africans became Christians through his influence than through that of any one missionary. He saw the danger that a church could concentrate so much on 'plant' that missionary giving suffered. Tony never took his eye off the need to support world mission, and urged that *B for the G* – as it became known – should draw in 'new money', and not divert anyone's current giving.

He saw, furthermore, that good premises were necessary to give an appropriate venue for people to be trained. It was most important, he felt, not to underestimate the time that it takes for new thought patterns to be formed, and hence for a biblical worldview to take root in a person's thinking. He longed to see more missionaries coming out of St Nicholas in years to come; to see Contact members receive the training they needed to stand for their faith in the increasingly tough thought-world of school and college; and to see church members thinking through the ways their faith applied to their work. The undercroft would give the premises for this. Putting hard cash into this project was a spiritual investment with global possibilities. For everyone to grasp this was vital. There would be a great deal of opposition to 'spending money on ourselves' and 'not sending it overseas instead'. Tony Wilmot's experience, credibility, availability and willingness were surely God-given for that time and that message. ✣

Chapter 5

Leading up to the big decision

No one can nail a date when St Nicholas, Sevenoaks finally resolved to go ahead with the undercroft option. The PCC meeting on 7 July 1990 is the point in history when a resolution was passed deciding to go forward. But these things are not so simple. If the church family did not get behind the plan financially, it would need to be reviewed. Also, the Bishop of Rochester, through his Diocesan Chancellor, would be the one to grant the Faculty.[1] So the PCC decision was only a step in a process, and that process was to last six years.

But even taking all these parties and processes into account, the picture is incomplete. For God was at work in people's lives – at times remarkably so; at other times almost imperceptibly. As the Rector, and churchwardens, and Tony Wilmot, and others closely involved in the planning pressed on, God gave them the sheer perseverance they needed. And as they and others in the church prayed, God heard their prayers, and slowly, steadily, changed hearts and attitudes.

What will history say?

How will local historians chronicle hopes and plans for this medieval building at the south end of the High Street in decades to come? That will depend entirely on who writes the history. To onlookers, this project consisted only in bricks and mortar, diggers and archaeology, permissions and contractors. But that analysis leaves too much unsaid. The whole purpose of the project was to create facilities to bring honour to Jesus Christ. It was a spiritual project, and could be truly perceived only with that purpose in view.

what will history say? It depends on who writes the history

Michael Baughen had warned that there would be

disappointments along the way, sometimes crushing ones. It is in such situations, he said, that our attitude to the Bible is put to the test. If this is God's Word for his world for all time, and if it is true, and 'sufficient' then we will be able to draw strength from it.[2] That 'very major promise' to which the Bishop had referred on his visit to St Nick's in 1989 was to prove a source of hope and stability throughout the whole process. The apostle Paul's letter to the church in Rome was another place in the Bible which people found themselves turning to over and over again. Paul linked suffering with perseverance and character-building, and with hope.[3] He put difficult and sometimes very painful experiences into a broader perspective, the eternal dimension.

Time to get on

Having waited since the 1960s for the right time to go ahead, at last it seemed that this had come. The church needed to pray: to pray for a willingness to give large sums of money, and then to give even more; to pray for minds to be changed where those in authority were reluctant to grant needed permissions; to pray for the Thomsons, the churchwardens, the treasurer, and the administrator, who were all under pressure.

No one wanted to be so preoccupied with the building work that the 'real' ministry of the church became neglected. Throughout the whole process of weighing the possibilities and making decisions, the two emphases of church life remained – Bible teaching and evangelism. And prayer for the whole life of the church was not to be sidelined by prayer for the building project.

Any large project involves simultaneous action on several fronts, and careful co-ordination of each of the different areas of activity. While the PCC retained ultimate responsibility, much of the work was delegated to a building committee and, in due course, to the Project Director. Later on, as the crucial final decision-making phase approached, Paul Batchelor, by that stage the treasurer, asked Miles to a create a Finance Advisory Group to bring together members of the church family with deep experience in banking, finance and legal matters. These groups were, in a real sense, on the front line, and their members shouldered a heavy load.

A note sent by Miles to the building committee in December 1990 summed things up well:

> May I share with you how the last 10 days have highlighted the need to press on with *Building for the Gospel?*
>
> **Parish Hall**: several people have pointed out the very limited daytime parking. We can squeeze only 10 or 11 cars on to the forecourt. South Park car park costs 30p for two hours. Recently a mum on the fringe of things gave up and went home when she was trying to get to Mum & Co as she couldn't park her car.
>
> For the special coffee morning on 11 December, car-parking again was a problem. Around 70-80 came. One person bringing a friend ended up parking in the Rectory as nearer car parks were all full. This does not make us 'user-friendly'.
>
> **Crèche:** There are 31 on the roll! That's great, but some parents are deciding not to leave their babies as it is such a squeeze. As a temporary expedient, the clergy can move out of the vestry on Sunday mornings, and take over the choir area, though this is not ideal. We can't lose new families.
>
> **Mum & Co:** The Christmas Party brought 95 children and babies. That is a marvellous link into the town. Please pray that Sara and her team may be able to build on this – for the gospel. We need to help people make the connection between the Parish Hall and St Nicholas, so people at Mum & Co come to where the gospel is taught.
>
> I'm not sure how we pass round this information, and so help a growing number in our church family to see the urgency of the issue. At the same time, let's thank God for the problems of *life*!

The issues were real. A cynical observer might interpret the concern to keep families as a way of ensuring longer-term financial support for the church. It is a poor reflection on things if people see the church as 'always asking for money'. Too often it is caricatured in that way. St Nicholas at this stage was in great need of money if the undercroft was to be achieved, but the desire to keep families in the church and to draw in more families through Mum & Co had no bearing on financial considerations.

Logo, brochures, video, scale model

Communication with the church family was vital. It was the lifeblood of the whole process, second only to prayer. Doris Colgate, a former pupil of Lady Boswell's School, and a contemporary of Tony Wilmot in the Contact group of the 1930s, has worshipped at St Nick's all her life. In her retirement, she combined stewarding at Knole House for the National Trust with voluntary work in the church office. Her willing spirit and sheer diligence were behind many of the brochures and updates which kept the church family in the picture. These were printed by Tony Jennings, one of the churchwardens. High value was placed on information not drying up. Monthly updates went only to the church family; others went out less frequently to all who lived in the parish. And Judith Cribb, who had previously worked in Public Relations for Littlewoods Stores, ensured a steady flow of news releases to the *Sevenoaks Chronicle*.

A local businessman designed a logo for the undercroft to be used on mugs and car stickers as well as on the brochures. These were all ways of raising the profile of *B for the G* and keeping it in people's minds. A video was specially commissioned, showing the urgent need for space, and featuring voices and faces from the church family. This helped bring home the need in a new way. Robert Potter had trodden similar paths before with other churches, and he suggested having a scale model made. Ron Harper from Southampton, with his gift for converting the two-dimensional into the three-dimensional, had constructed such models for the Sarum Partnership on several occasions. For two years the problems had been talked about. Now people could see the video, and grasp the difficulties. For two years a possible solution had been shown on paper, and on the overhead projector. Now they could actually imagine themselves 'under the church'. The model and the video circled Sevenoaks at a series of 'at homes'. It was no longer just a hypothetical solution to a problem: it could become a reality.

Moving towards the formal launch

At the same time the search started for the right man for the job of Project Director. This would be a full-time position for at least three years. Already the clergy team was working at full stretch; in order to maintain their pastoral ministry, they would need to be kept free from distraction. The Project Director would have a critical and wide-ranging role, which would include public relations, press relations, liaison with the contractors, and the general smooth-running of church life while the work was in progress. Roles like that are not easy to fill.

David Milton-Thompson preached on the last Sunday of May 1991 from Luke's gospel, on the cost of following Jesus. He and his wife, Bea, had been missionaries in China until they were expelled by the communists in 1952. Back in Britain, they faced the choice of staying at home, or going somewhere else overseas. Undeterred by the prospect of learning another new language and trying to understand another new – and very different – culture, they went to Kaloleni in south east Kenya, to run a hospital. As David taught from the passage that day, he spoke with authority, and his own life gave him credibility. 'No one who puts his hand to the plough and looks back is fit for service in the kingdom of God.' We as a church had put our 'hand to the plough'. We were not unaware of the cost. We must not look back.

The following week saw the formal launch of the project. The Parish Hall was decorated and tables carefully laid for a lunch to which some 55 church and civic dignitaries were invited. The menu was in the hands of Marilynn Sowerby, who masterminded catering arrangements throughout *B for the G*, and the atmosphere was warm and positive.

In his address, the Bishop of Rochester, Michael Turnbull, said that the time had come for Sevenoaks to catch up with the rest of the world. He had doubtless sensed both caution and conservatism in the correspondence columns of the local newspaper. At this meeting the video had its 'world premier', and the scale model was on display.

During that week there were six special presentations using the video and the model, with an average attendance of 180 people. Here people heard not only the plans, but the reasons behind *B for the G*. Each evening, a group met to pray while these events took place. The undercroft was to be dug out for the glory of God. The new premises were to be used for his glory.

It would be four years before the project was completed and through that time the huge initial effort would need to be sustained.

'Don't give unless you can give cheerfully'

On 16 June 1991 Andrew Cornes, vicar of All Saints, Crowborough, preached at both services. In the morning he took Acts 4 where the apostles Peter and John were brought before the local Jewish leaders and imprisoned overnight for what they were preaching. The local Christians prayed for courage to speak openly about what they believed, and their prayers were answered in a dramatic way. Andrew asked what St Nick's expected from their own praying. It was a helpful question. In the evening he preached from 2 Corinthians 9, where the apostle Paul describes the godly way of giving: 'Whoever sows sparingly will also reap sparingly; whoever sows generously will also reap generously. Each man should give what he has decided in his heart to give, not reluctantly or under compulsion, for God loves a cheerful giver.'[4] The media pundits may tell us how successful an able orator can be in exhorting people to give. But for such serious-minded and long-term giving as would be necessary, more than oratory was needed. Andrew depended on the authority of Scripture in what he said, and on the Holy Spirit to take the message home to people's hearts.

the huge initial effort would need to be sustained

Throughout the whole process of raising funds, no huge thermometer appeared outside the church to tell the public how far there was to go. And special events had no side agendas of drawing in people in order to increase the financial support base. Every effort was made to ensure that people did not feel pressurised to give money for the undercroft. It was felt that this was a personal matter, and a serious one, and an issue for church members to resolve with their families, or on their own, before God. Few outside the church would have known that Miles never saw how much anyone had given. That information was strictly confidential to Paul Batchelor as treasurer and Judith Robinson as covenant secretary, and their team; and it has remained so. In whatever way people responded to the undercroft – whether enthusiastically, sympathetically, neutrally or antagonistically – Miles was their pastor, and nothing should be allowed to affect that, or to be perceived to affect it.

Landmarks in time

The church family was invited to pledge money for the undercroft a fortnight after Andrew Cornes's visit, on the last Sunday of June 1991. However, on the principle that the leaders should lead, the PCC made their pledges first, and the total pledged was announced on the Sunday in between. It was £291,000. This was a wonderful start, and a way of dispelling publicly any fears there might have been that the PCC was not united.

Sunday 30 June came, and people placed their envelopes in the boxes as they arrived for the service. After these had been brought to the front of the church, and received with prayer, Miles preached. The passage was from Philippians 3, which set in stark contrast any merit on this earth with 'the surpassing greatness of knowing Christ Jesus'. Miles simply expounded what Paul wrote.

The evening service followed a similar pattern, with the curate, Johnny Juckes, preaching on Isaiah 40. This brought a powerful reminder that God can be trusted. Halfway through the service, Colin and Hazel Maunsell, home briefly from Ethiopia, were interviewed about their work in that land. It was fitting to express commitment to them on this particular Sunday. The undercroft could not be allowed to preoccupy a missionary-minded church. That service closed with Timothy Dudley-Smith's hymn 'Lord, for the years'. Bishop Timothy and his family had worshipped at St Nicholas in the 1960s, and were remembered with affection.

The Holy Spirit had evidently been at work in people's lives. Many went home with joy in their hearts. They had been blessed through their giving. And more money arrived over the course of the next day. By the following evening, £829,000 had been pledged by around forty per cent of the church family. This sum of money expressed massive support, and confirmed the Lord's own blessing on the whole endeavour. What a landmark!

Monday 1 July 1991 brought things another step forward too. News came from Brigadier Ian Dobbie that he could take on the role of Project Director from the following spring. Ian was Chairman of the Soldiers'and Airmen's Scripture Readers' Association. He had served overseas in the Royal Engineers, and as an instructor both at Sandhurst and at the RAF

The Maunsells' story

Colin and Hazel Maunsell live in Addis Ababa in Ethiopia. Hazel's links with St Nick's began when her parents moved to the nearby village of Otford and her father became a lay reader at the church.

Hazel spent three years working among students in the Midlands universities with what is now the Universities and Colleges Christian Fellowship (UCCF) and after this, went out to Ethiopia where she started to learn Amharic, and to identify with the Ethiopian culture. Colin had already been in Ethiopia for some twelve years by that time. This country is one of the oldest known nations in the world, and the Ethiopian Orthodox Church goes back to the 4th century. In living memory it has seen not only famine, drought and wars, but a Marxist revolution under which Christians were persecuted and churches closed.

Since 1991 there has been unprecedented freedom in the country for Christian worship and witness. The Maunsells' major task is to produce Amharic literature which will help Ethiopian Christians grow in their understanding of the Bible. They have completed a course of daily Bible studies called *Every day with God* which goes through the Bible in four years, and are working on a series of 'Pillar books' which explain the central truths of the faith. They are also revising and expanding the Amharic Bible Dictionary first edited by Colin in 1980. Hazel has produced story books in a new format which tell the gospel in parables, and in a way which is especially suitable for country people.

Colin teaches courses locally and further afield, and is able to use the experience he gains to devise materials to help other teachers. Both he and Hazel frequently write articles for Christian magazines. Hazel's articles on marriages and families in the Bible are currently forming the basis for new books. In all their writing, Colin and Hazel work closely with Ethiopian scholars.

Alongside the literature work, Colin has preaching opportunities at the Anglican Chaplaincy, and Hazel leads a meeting for Bible study in the Fistula Hospital in Addis, for patients and staff. Their home is open to many in different kinds of need, and people of all ages come to it for Bible teaching, from children upwards.

The Maunsells are members of Crosslinks, a mission agency based in Lewisham, southeast London, which has workers in countries in Europe, Asia and Africa.

Staff College, and had held office in the Directorate of Manning, in the Ministry of Defence and as Deputy Chief of Staff of an Armoured Division. A military career like that may seem an unusual training for working in a church, but in the providence of God, St Nick's had a man with an unusual range of gifts and experience to bring to an unusual role.

That same day the Thomsons received a letter from a Christian friend urging them not to lose heart, and reminding them of the long journey of the children of Israel to reach their promised land after escaping from Egypt. Letters like this bringing greetings and encouragement were deeply appreciated, and they kept coming – often arriving at the same time as a disheartening letter. A few days later an envelope came from a woman whose husband was ill, promising £10 per month in cash. To receive notes like that was very humbling. These envelopes on the doormat meant more than the writers ever knew.

By 4 July 1991 total pledges had risen to £845,000. By the end of the month they stood at £965,000.

The building committee and PCC had agreed that plans be set in motion to proceed with detailed designs and the preparation of tender documents once £1,000,000 had been pledged. Another Update went out to the church family. While there was a tremendous sense of excitement around, there were still some who felt uneasy about the undercroft. It was a period of ups and downs. While some in the church family went without a holiday or delayed changing their cars, or took on extra work to be able to give more to the project, a few left the church, feeling a big mistake was being made.

It had always been clear that there was no obligation to support the undercroft financially. Those who felt the money should be going overseas were specifically invited to give to the Missionary Fund rather than to the building project. But if in the end people resolved to leave and to worship elsewhere, then that decision, though sad, had to be respected. In each case, they were

a few left the church, feeling a big mistake was being made assured of a welcome back, should they feel it right to return, at any stage.

By September 1991 the £1,000,000 milestone was reached.

Staying on track

Sunday by Sunday, the teaching of Scripture addressed issues in people's minds. That summer Miles was preaching a series on the Songs of Ascent – the psalms sung by the people of Israel as they travelled to Jerusalem for special feasts. They were psalms of pilgrimage from which strong parallels could be drawn. In Israel then, as in Sevenoaks, a group of God's people were on a journey. By the end of July 1991, Miles reached Psalm 133, with its clear plea for unity. Unity in the gospel was of far greater importance than anything else. Whatever people felt about the undercroft, St Nick's must guard its unity.

some people still had genuine questions about the costs

Some people still had genuine unresolved questions about the costs, and the ethics of 'spending money on ourselves', and these needed to be addressed. Having lived for so long in Africa, Tony Wilmot had seen poverty in the raw. As Chairman of the missionary committee, he could not ignore the real and pressing needs of other places in the world. In August that year he preached on Jesus's own words: 'The poor you will always have with you.' The undercroft project presented an unusual opportunity to give sacrificially for God's glory, and the time to give was now. The Lord was not here devaluing kindness to the poor; that would be to deny the character of God, who is full of compassion. Again, it was the teaching of Scripture being applied to the questions of the moment.

If the Bible is our guide for all that we believe, and all that we do, it has to remain in the forefront of our thinking. That is the essence of what it means to be an evangelical church. And the preaching on Sundays and daily Bible reading in homes played a very significant role in keeping the project on course, in proportion and – all importantly – focused on its spiritual goal.

When the going gets tough

Correspondence continued to appear regularly in the *Sevenoaks Chronicle*. It came from Sevenoaks residents who felt the money should have gone instead to the less-privileged here or overseas, and from others who felt the church was being ruined by any attempt to modernise it. Life would certainly have been far easier without any building project at all. Again and again, what kept the momentum going was Scripture's central thrust, traced from Genesis to Revelation, of a missionary God with a missionary heart and an ever-contemporary message. It did not mean that no one ever lost heart. But that was what drove people back to redouble their praying when things got tough. That was what counted.

As autumn drew on, God again and again brought new resolve to those most closely involved, through their own Bible reading. As English Heritage and the Royal Fine Arts Commission examined plans closely, it was evident that there would be problems. The building committee did not know whether to laugh or cry when English Heritage made a counter proposal: an undercroft of smaller proportions beneath the church car park!

Bishop Michael Baughen was closely supportive of Miles and Sara throughout. In God's providence, he had been appointed as the House of Lords representative to groups like English Heritage. At a particularly difficult stage of negotiations, he found himself sharing a taxi with Robert Potter in London, and they talked about the undercroft. He was due to meet with a senior member of English Heritage the following week on behalf of the Lords, and said he would take the opportunity of raising the matter at the same time. Yet again it seemed that the course of human events was diverted. In what had appeared a stalemate, they were able to reach a compromise with which everyone was happy. The external ramp in the original design would go, but some internal features which had proved contentious would stay, and a wide lift could provide for the needs of the elderly and disabled.

yet again it seemed the course of human events was diverted

As if to confirm God's

blessing, an anonymous gift arrived the following week through a Luxemburg bank for £24,000.

As 1992 began, the Sunday preaching focused on the book of Joshua and the theme chosen for the year was a phrase from Joshua 1:9 – God's words to a new leader who was following in the footsteps of the mighty Moses –'Be strong and courageous.'

Hurdles

The Sevenoaks District Council posted a planning notice inviting comments through the usual channels. Eight letters were written, five in favour of the plans and three against. At its meeting on 30 January 1992, the Sevenoaks District Council took no more than three minutes to pass the plans unanimously. Around the same time, a citation was placed on the church door, asking any objectors to put their arguments in writing to the Chancellor of the Diocese within 17 days. Three people did this, but none wanted to proceed to a formal objection, so avoiding the possibility of a consistory court.

But there were more hurdles ahead. Over the following week Miles received letters from unhappy church members, urging a change of plan even at this stage, and other letters were written to the Registrar of the Diocese. If the Chancellor's permission was delayed because of disaffected church members, prices could go up considerably. The building committee and PCC were urged to pray. On top of everything else, a visit from the Fire Officer brought further problems. He insisted on the need for an external staircase. If this proved non-negotiable, it was highly likely that English Heritage would object. Every delay like this was potentially costing a great deal of money.

On 13 March 1992 Chris Webb, a member of the building committee, faxed a cutting from *The Times* that morning to the church office. Under the title 'Rise in sales of new homes reported' it read:

> Ministers anxious for evidence of the long-awaited upturn in the economy will today take comfort from a report suggesting sales activity in the housing market is beginning to show a marked improvement...Mr David Holliday, President of the Housing Builders' Federation, said there was positive indication that purchaser interest in new homes was being converted into

sales. He went on to predict that the housing market would now begin to move forward strongly throughout the remainder of 1992.

It was typical of several brief reports appearing in the press. The country was moving out of recession. It was important to act soon.

Again, people were urged to make the matter a priority in their prayers. Eventually English Heritage agreed that an external fire exit staircase would be acceptable as long as it was not visible from the road; the architect was able to incorporate this constraint into the design.

The budget estimate was now £2,250,000. But with that came the good news of planning permission for the Parish Hall to be demolished and for flats to be built on the site.[5] This, too, had been achieved only after overcoming opposition from conservationists. The post that week also brought more letters from church members who were unsure or unhappy about developments.

By now all needed planning permissions had been granted, but along with them arrived a condition: namely that the church should cover the costs of archaeologists working on the site. This could add £100,000 to the bill.

A special thanksgiving service was held at the end of April, but some came with mixed feelings. The Chantry next door to the church had come on the market, and a few felt this would be a preferable alternative, even if it meant a very late change of plan. However the Chantry was an ancient building, and would need a lot of renovation to make it suitable for meeting rooms. And in any case, it was far too small.

News of permission to demolish the Parish Hall had been received with some ambivalence by the Campaigners. They loved the hall for all the reasons that others found it unsuitable! The Sevenoaks branch of this national uniformed movement started in 1954 and for over 40 years has been led by a dedicated group of helpers including the Wood family. Its Junos (six -11) and Inters (11-15) were meeting in the hall on Monday evenings and appreciated the liberty they had there for rough and tumble games. It has always been a thriving group with excellent links to local schools.

If the hall were to be sold, it would be a big loss for this group as the low-ceilinged undercroft would put too many restrictions on their activities.

The PCC made a commitment to look for equally suitable premises for the Campaigners to use. While the matter of a venue for Campaigners remained unresolved, there was a feeling of unhappiness among some in the church, which expressed itself as a deep sense of unease about the whole undercroft project. As a result, a handful of people left, and others took a long time to recover. Campaigners has always included children from totally unchurched backgrounds, and has been a way of drawing them in to hear the Christian gospel. No one wanted to lose this ministry. It was a vital part of church life.

In a last effort to win the confidence of those who were disaffected, a final open meeting was planned for questions and answers. After this, the matter would be considered closed. It turned out to be a good meeting, with just over 20 people present, and everyone having the chance to

the Holy Spirit was changing minds and attitudes

speak and to feel they had been heard. While members of the building committee fielded the questions, a group of wives met to pray in the Rectory. At the end of the evening an envelope was handed in – a new pledge to replace one which had been rescinded earlier. The Holy Spirit was at work, changing hearts, changing minds, changing attitudes.

Hudson Taylor, the pioneer missionary to China, had founded the China Inland Mission in 1865 with '£10 in the bank and all the promises of God'.[6] He wrote later, 'God's work done in God's way will not lack supply.' Taylor knew what it meant to depend on God, and he weathered every possible criticism, pressing on in the face of it. That kind of dependence on God was vital to progress in *B for the G* and should not be allowed to diminish. The weeknight prayer meeting was an anchor in church life, and monthly Saturday morning prayer times for the project also became a regular feature. Learning to 'work with God', as Michael Baughen had described it, was central. ❧

How the money was raised

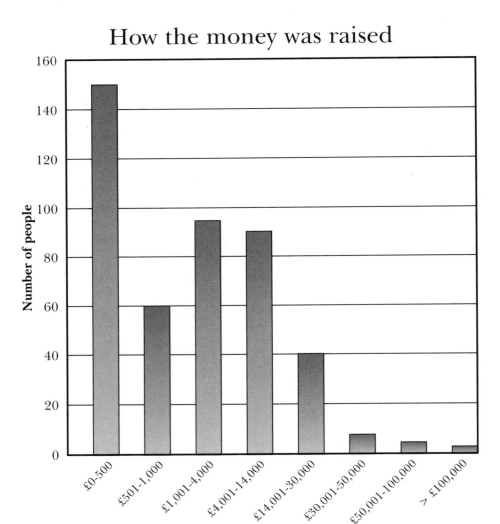

Size of total gift

The size of donation to qualify for additional benefit through Gift Aid was reduced by the government in April 1992 from £600 to £400, and further reduced in April 1993 to £250. This was a significant help in 'Building for the Gospel'

Chapter 6

Two million pounds is a lot of money!

Faith and finance are completely intertwined in a story like this. Here was a church with around 350 adults in services on any given Sunday. Some earned substantial salaries and spent their working days dealing with finance. For them, it was easier to put the figure in perspective. But they were in the minority. Middle income families made up the largest numbers. One can imagine some of the thoughts going through their minds as they wanted to play their part and wondered how things might be juggled. Then there were pensioners, young singles and newly-married couples, many with more limited incomes. A few of the longest-standing members had never owned their own homes, or through the change in government policy had only recently purchased them from the Council. To see this project through, everyone needed to pull together; to contribute what they could, indeed *all* they could. The church was a family, and there was no distinction in that regard between those in professions, and those in more modestly-paid employment.

The church is 'ours'

The Stag Theatre, 200 yards from St Nicholas, had just completed major refurbishment costing nearly £3m. Developing the theatre's facilities was achieved largely through the single-minded effort of its founder, and the combination of pressure and persuasion she was able to bring to bear on the discretionary spending of Sevenoaks District Council. It was a huge achievement, and it has provided the town with a theatre and cinema to serve for generations.[1] But a theatre is different from a church. The District Council had neither the funds nor the reason to pay for the undercroft. And to have done so would, anyway, have denied St Nick's members the privilege and joy of sacrificial giving.

The idea of hiring a professional fundraiser was considered. With such a huge sum in view, it might have seemed sensible to hire people with experience in this 'art'. However, after contacting one or two fund-raisers, and on the advice of those who had undertaken similar projects elsewhere, it was decided not to do this. The church family would need to give most of the money themselves, and not to rely on trusts or high-profile fund-raising events, since neither of these could be expected to make more than a minor contribution to a sum of this size. People living in the parish would be invited to give, but the matter would be handled in a low-key way. Largely, the finance would come from the church family. And it was felt that blessing would come through that, as members learned more about God's generosity to them as they gave. Through this act of obedience, they would prove that 'he is no man's debtor'. This was not to condemn other Christians for handling their appeals more publicly. But it was the agreed way ahead for St Nick's.

it became a topic of dinner party conversation across town

The *Sevenoaks Chronicle* covered the story well, and kept townspeople in the picture as to progress. Here was a seven-figure building fund, and the first figure was not a one. The sheer magnitude of the amount was news in itself, and it became a topic of dinner party conversation across the town. Public money is one thing. This was personal money. Wasn't it taking religion a bit too far?

Getting a right perspective

Paul Batchelor, as treasurer for *B for the G*, encouraged people to put the sum in perspective. It should be seen, he said, in relation to the value of homes and cars owned by church members. The cost of the original building, in real terms, must have been vast; this was a way of continuing and preserving what our forbears had done. It would be a place for gospel witness over the next thousand years, if the Lord did not return in the meantime.

With careful management of funds, compound interest was to accrue to a significant sum. Where people came on board early with their gifts, or committed themselves to regular giving over a long period of time, there was significant benefit. The income from tax recovery was also very large.

Effective giving

There are both practical and spiritual lessons to learn from a project like this:

- All gifts are important and valuable. No gift is too small to consider. All promote a sense of involvement and commitment.

- Sustained, sacrificial giving is the most effective. Regular giving becomes part of one's way of life. The sums donated earn interest, and often attract tax relief. The combined effect is very striking. In this project, the combined income from interest and tax recoveries was over £500,000.

- The most tax-effective way is giving through the Gift Aid scheme (for lump sums) and through deeds of covenant, or through institutions like the Charities Aid Foundation (CAF).

- For individuals and families, it is important to plan and budget for giving. It may help to set the sum aside in a separate account. In that way it does not get diverted unintentionally.

- If you cannot afford to give much money, give your abilities, and don't underestimate the value of giving time to prayer.

- Be a cheerful giver.

- Remember that all we have comes from God. We are merely giving back a small part of that.

- God rewards our giving many times over, spiritually.

Understandably, perhaps, some held back. They were not confident that sufficient money would be raised. Once they saw the level of giving rise, they, too, would give. In a major project like this, the balance between those who will give in faith and those who want to see success round the corner first is critical. 'Lord, I believe. Help my unbelief,' must have been the essence of many people's prayers as they filled in their covenants and wrote their cheques before it became definite that the Diocesan Chancellor would give permission for the project to go ahead. And they probably became the major prayer force in asking for others to be moved from scepticism to risk-taking faith.

As the offering is brought to the front of the church each Sunday, the leader of the service prays, 'All things come from you, O Lord,' and the congregation responds, 'And of your own have we given you.' These are lines taken from a prayer of King David back in the tenth century BC. They emphasize that everything in heaven and on earth belongs to God. Even we ourselves. All we give him is only part of what he has given us. As that truth seeps more and more into our thinking and our planning, it becomes more natural to think realistically about financial matters. We are stewards, not owners. And we must be faithful stewards.

It is a false hope to think that presently unknown trusts 'out there' will somehow save a congregation from having to give money for building projects. Less than £20,000 came from outside sources for the undercroft in the end. As one church member said, 'This is really just housekeeping. *Of course* we expected to pay for it ourselves.'

We have the money!

There is a popular cartoon with a minister giving announcements in a Sunday service. It runs like this:

Minister: The good news is that we already have all the money we need for our building work.

(The cartoonist shows the faces of the congregation. Everyone looks pleased, relieved, assured. Someone else has spared them from having to give. Wonderful to hear! But things change in the next frame...)

Minister: But the bad news is that it is still in your bank accounts.

We laugh because it is funny. That kind of caricature has a wonderful simplistic charm. But an approach like that will never draw the hard cash it is looking for. There is a world of difference between what is sometimes called 'the ethics of guilt' and 'the ethics of gratitude'. If several, even many, people are embarrassed into writing a cheque for £50 or even for £200, then that might mend a leaking roof or replace rotting boards. That is 'the ethics of guilt' in action. It sets out to appease consciences, and gives a

there is a difference between 'ethics of guilt' and 'ethics of gratitude'

sense of 'having done one's bit'. But the ethics of guilt will never be imaginative and creative. It will not, it cannot, create the fitting new premises for corporate worship and for evangelism which churches up and down the country need today. How different from the ethics of gratitude, where giving springs out of thankfulness to God, truly *believing* that all we have comes from him, and being thankful that we, ourselves, 'have been bought with a price' by Christ's death on a cross. That makes all the difference in the world. For how can we give him enough in return? And how can we not give with joy?

The diagram on p58 shows how individuals or families contributed to *B for the G*. It also shows the joint effort of those with large incomes, those with middle incomes and those with smaller incomes, of pensioners, and of young people with pocket money. This was a spiritual enterprise, not a competition for the size of gift, and people were encouraged to give cheerfully, and as they were able.

Jesus is very interested in giving

The story of 'the widow's mite' is well known. Jesus was very interested in giving, and in Mark's gospel we read that he sat himself down right opposite the place in the temple where the offerings were left, and watched the crowd putting their money into the temple treasury.

Many rich people threw in large amounts. But a poor widow came and threw in two very small copper coins, worth only a fraction of a penny. Calling his disciples to him, Jesus said, 'I tell you the truth, this poor widow has put into the treasury more than all the others. They all gave out of their wealth; but she, out of her poverty, put in everything – all she had to live on.[2]

These few verses, which have travelled down the centuries, go right to the heart of the issue. Some of the most faithful giving in the course of the project was from those of limited means who gave what they could afford in cash in envelopes, weekly or monthly, over several years. Motivation is everything in God's sight. These people gave out of their love for him. Creating the undercroft would require that a lot of people also gave substantial sums 'out of their wealth'. How vitally important, in a spiritual sense, that these greatly-needed major donors should be giving for the right reasons too.

Passing a milestone and facing up to a challenge

After the initial appeal, the total pledges crept up only slowly, and at times seemed to be stuck. At the same time, the detailed designs were being developed and as these took shape, it appeared that costs might escalate. In September 1991 the £1,000,000 mark had been reached. The pledges levelled after that, and crept up only slowly over the following 18 months. This period brought feelings of uncertainty and at times, for some, even despair. Then, by May 1993, the total promised had risen to £1,200,000, and more than half that sum had already been given. This was another wonderful milestone. But it was still not enough to move forward. The Diocesan Chancellor felt unable to give permission to proceed without a substantially-greater sum of money actually in the bank. The nature of the project meant it could not be halted midway: what would happen if the rest of the giving did not materialise? The recession was still affecting many people, and those with savings had suffered a significant loss over the previous two years; others had lost their jobs.

Now the 'milestone' brochure arrived in every member's home. How would people react? Some were already feeling the effects of 'giving fatigue'; others who had been hesitant earlier were even more hesitant now after the economic beating they had gone through. Of the 520 people on the Electoral Roll, just over 300 had given.

The brochure was written jointly by David Brewster, Legal Director for IMRO, who chaired the Finance Advisory Group, and Paul Batchelor. It laid out the matter clearly:

> God has faithfully met our prayers. He has removed all other obstacles from our path. Now he is challenging us to make some sacrifices, and to return to him part of the gifts he has given to us. We should welcome the challenge. The time has come to put doubts and division behind us, and to unite in the cause of the One whom we all desire to serve, and whose gospel we wish to proclaim more effectively here in Sevenoaks. *It is not a matter for others, but for each and every one of us.*
>
> • Of those who have already given generously, we ask, can you do more?
> • Of those who have made a start, we ask, can you go further?
> • Of those who have waited, we ask, is not now the time to start?
> • Of those who have doubted, we ask, can you now see these signs of God's will and join us?
>
> It has perhaps fallen to us to have the privilege to equip St Nicholas for many generations to come. Two years ago we were moved to pledge almost a million pounds for this cause. Most of this is now being faithfully contributed. Please pray that, in a few weeks' time, we will be similarly moved so that, together, with God's help, we can do the same again.

The leaflet closed with the increasingly familiar words of the apostle Paul to the Christians in Ephesus: 'Now to him who is able to do immeasurably more than all we ask or imagine, according to his power that is at work within us, to him be glory in the church and in Christ Jesus throughout all generations, for ever and ever!' Sunday 20 June 1993 was the next Pledge and Thanksgiving Sunday. Everyone knew that God's help was needed. Over £1,000,000 was still to be found, and that was immeasurably more than many in the church family dared to imagine could be forthcoming.

The PCC again led the way, a week earlier, with pledges amounting to £250,000. (This brought total PCC pledges for the whole project to £500,000. That kind of leadership was very humbling.) Paul Batchelor rang the Thomsons late in the evening of 20 June. It looked as if the total pledges that day had brought the amount up to £575,000. Janet called the next morning to say it had risen to £580,000. If a loan could be secured against the value of the Parish Hall, there was sufficient to proceed.

There was still a cash-flow problem to overcome. The building programme would last two years; the giving would spread over seven years. To delay the start would risk rising costs. This problem was overcome largely by interest-free loans, again from church members. These totalled over £500,000 at their peak. But the Diocese also helped with a loan, and the church's bank generously provided bridging finance without calling for formal security. The branch manager at the time remarked, 'I can see there is good faith in this project!'

Stories, stories

Everyone who has used the popular Time Manager system will know this celebrated question and answer:

Q: How do you eat an elephant?
A: Bit by bit.

Facile for executives who construct their lives around its eight-point diary system? Not at all. We must all break down our elephant-sized tasks and, with God's help, tackle them bit by bit, with the human-sized energy he has given us. Hudson Taylor moved from 'Impossible' through 'Difficult' to 'Done' in just this way. He walked along the sands in Brighton on 25 June 1865 praying for '24 skilful, willing workers' to go to China. Two dozen people, who as yet had no Chinese language, to make an impact on a massive country, with an ancient culture steeped in 'isms' and folk religion! It sounded impossible. But this was the first step in taking the gospel of Christ to its inland provinces. China was the size of a whole herd of Time Manager's notional elephants, not just one. But two people for each inland province so far without any missionary, and two for Mongolia was a start. Similarly, two million pounds was a huge sum. But looked at 'bit by bit' it could come into focus – for everyone.

China was the size of a whole herd of Time Manager's elephants

As with many churches, the St Nick's congregation includes several wives whose husbands do not share their faith and commitment. It would be wrong for those wives to put pressure on the family budget for a project like this. Two moving stories of people in this situation were to emerge. One such wife received an unexpected legacy, which she felt able to give without affecting the family budget. Another found herself with a tax repayment she was not anticipating. Again, this was something she could give. These were gifts from the heart. Coming as they did from wives wanting to observe the biblical pattern of not antagonising their husbands, and yet at the same time wanting to give, they were specially meaningful. It was as if God had provided the means, in each case.

There was a lot of imaginative thinking about how to raise money. Ian Dobbie invited people to look out 'the redundant wealth' in their lofts and garages, and an auction was held in the Parish Hall which raised £9,000. Derek Hodge of Ibbett Moseley, a long-established firm of estate agents on the High Street, gave an afternoon of his time to act as auctioneer.

The *St Nicholas Cookbook* was launched in 1992 with all sorts of recipes including the very popular five-minute all-tinned 'quick bean stew', and various imports from Europe, Africa and Asia. Many churches have produced collections like this in a simple spiral binding. They are always a winner, especially when they draw in recipes from children and teenagers.

One church member gave £200 specifically for use as a 'talent fund'. Anyone could ask for money from this to invest in personal fundraising projects. It could cover, for example, ingredients for baking, or material for sewing.

- One of the young wives offered New Testament Greek lessons in her home.
- A group of older women made baby clothes, padded coat-hangers, cushion covers – each beautifully sewn.
- Students took up gardening and decorating in the vacations, and gave 20% of their earnings to the fund.
- A person with artistic gifts made Christmas cards.
- Another painted a watercolour of the church, from which a limited

collection of prints was sold.
- A third artist accepted commissions to do paintings of church members' houses.
- The choir gave a special concert.
- Centrepoint teenagers washed cars.
- Smaller children saved from their pocket money, and collected coins in Smartie tubes.

These all-important initiatives drew in everyone who wanted to give, but perhaps could not pledge part of their regular income. There will never be a comprehensive list of everything that was done. Many stories are known only to the givers. The small children's Smartie tubes raised a magnificent total of £75. That must have meant some real sacrificial giving from those kids. What children can't, in a split second, reel off sweets they would like to buy, or other things they want to do with their pocket money?

The base of giving grew wider and wider as people became more convinced of the need, and of the project's potential success.

In secular postmodern Britain, where so little credence is given to Christian principles in public morality, it is rather satisfying to note that the Inland Revenue was the 'number one' donor, through the generous provision of the government for covenanted charitable giving.

The final push

In May 1993 the PCC invited tenders for the building work. At the same time a detailed business plan was being prepared for the Diocesan Chancellor for the needed Faculty. This was delivered on its due date, 20 May, and a week later, the three competitive tenders came in. The most attractive offered potential savings of almost one third of a million pounds against the pre-tender budget! Was this a sign of God's blessing? During the course of construction, costs did escalate again, but they remained within the original budget estimates. They would not have done so without this substantial initial reduction.

However, the Chancellor was not yet ready to grant a Faculty. He did not feel he could rely on pledges, having known difficulties in other churches.

After the Thanksgiving and Commitment day of 20 June 1993, the gap between the estimated costs and the sum pledged had shrunk to £100,000; less than five per cent of the total. With bridging finance from the bank, interest free loans from within the church family, and a loan from the diocese, this gap could be closed. Excitement rose.

A revised business plan was hastily prepared. It demonstrated to the Chancellor the faithful record of giving over the previous two years, showing that, in the majority of cases, pledges had been honoured. It explained how the cash flow would work during construction, and set out the consequences of delays in going ahead. It had the unequivocal backing of the Finance Advisory Group, and demonstrated the depth of financial and business experience they had brought to bear. But the Chancellor still had questions.

The tenders would expire at noon on Friday 23 July. With the prospect of costs escalating, or even of having to re-tender, the pressure was on. A further letter was written that Wednesday evening, answering all the questions raised – about the profile of giving, and the number of people who had given to the project. It also sought to allay fears that some might have been coerced into pledging more than they could afford. Janet Batchelor delivered it personally to the Chancellor's home on the Thursday morning.

a rainbow showed God keeps his promises

At 10.00am on Friday, Miles received a call. The Diocesan Chancellor had agreed to grant the Faculty. There were only two hours left to spare. God had taken the church family 'right down to the wire'.

That Sunday evening, towards the end of the service, there was an enormous clap of thunder and simultaneous lightning. As the service closed, the sight of a striking rainbow served as a reminder that God keeps his promises. ✤

Chapter 7

The exile

This chapter is divided into three sections. First we look at leaving the church building for the contractors to move in; secondly at church life while the building work was being done; and thirdly at what was happening 'on site' at St Nicholas.

1: Leaving the church building

Just ten days after the Chancellor's permission had been received for the undercroft to go ahead, the church family of St Nicholas moved out. Linking their situation – rather tenuously – to that of the Jews who had been taken captive in Babylon, and were eventually allowed to return to Jerusalem to help rebuild its temple, the time of exclusion from the building was nicknamed 'the exile'.

The final services in St Nick's were held on 1 August 1993. It was bound to be a significant day for everyone. Some of the very elderly must have wondered if they would ever worship in the building again. The enthusiasm for the plans from this sector of the church family in particular had meant a great deal. They were likely to find it harder than others to worship in a school hall instead of a church building. But they just got on with it. The notice sheet that Sunday asked prayer for 68 members and leaders of Contact who were in Norfolk for their annual houseparty. That was a marvellous number of senior school pupils and students to take away. Could it grow further with the new facilities?

enthusiasm from the elderly meant a great deal

In the morning, Miles preached from 1 Samuel 7: 'The Philistine army had been routed, and Samuel wanted to mark a great victory. He did so by setting up a large stone, which was like a war memorial, but with one big difference. It didn't contain the names of the dead – those who had died in battle – but just one name, the name of the *living*, the living God who had helped them to win the victory. As we think of building for the gospel we can say, as Samuel did, "In everything has the Lord helped us".

'That Stone was a powerful reminder. As they looked at it, it would strengthen their trust in the Lord for the next challenge. We can look back and rejoice. We can look ahead and trust because "in everything has the Lord helped *us*" too.' Quoting from Joseph Hart's hymn, Miles finished: 'So we'll praise him for all that is past, and trust him for all that's to come.'

A crèche was arranged for the evening service, so that whole families could come if they wanted to. This was an historic day: the culmination of dreams and prayers over 30 years. The final hymn to be sung in the church before the exile took up from where Miles had finished in the morning as everyone stood to sing:

> How good is the God we adore,
> Our faithful, unchangeable friend
> Whose love is as great as his power,
> And knows neither measure nor end.

Then people all picked up a kneeler to carry it to the back of the church with them. This was a small help for the volunteer force who were to clear the building the next day, but it was also – and more importantly – a symbolic act. The whole church family was 'hands-on' in that earliest step of transforming the old St Nick's into what they had dreamed of, prayed for, and given for. Everyone then snaked up Six Bells Lane and on to the Parish Hall, where the singing of the hymn continued:

> For Christ is the first and the last;
> His Spirit will guide us safe home:
> We'll praise him for all that is past
> And trust him for all that's to come.

After committing to God in prayer all that lay ahead in this great 'adventure of faith', a large cake was cut and handed round. It had become a St Nick's tradition for all important 'occasions' to be marked in this way.

Surely this one qualified!

The following day, a group of volunteers under Ian Dobbie's direction cleared the church completely, apart from the pews. Richard Morgan and Guy Powell, both members of the church, who run a local removal business, were on hand with a van. Only one room not affected could be used for storage during the next 18 months. Everything else not needed for services would have to be packed into the attics or basement of the Parish Hall, or sold, or otherwise disposed of. Everything. And that included the floorboards. Valuables which were not needed in the interim period were stored in people's homes. It was a major job.

What happened to the pews

End to end, the pews would have stretched to about a furlong: an eighth of a mile of weighty, solid, local oak. Knowing the affection in which the building was held, the PCC resolved to give church members an opportunity to buy pews if they wanted to, before Ian arranged for the sale of those which were left. To price them within the reach of any member, the three-seaters went for £100 each. Providentially, the number of shorter pews and the number of people wanting them matched exactly.

One brave townsman took the risk of buying a 17 foot pew to squeeze into his family sitting room. It took five men to lift it into the back of a lorry, and the only way to get it all in was to jam it diagonally at 45 degrees. As it was unloaded, there was more than a little apprehension as to whether the scheme would work. It did, just. All the other longer pews were sold to Pew Corner in Godalming, Surrey, a firm which cuts them down for sale into more manageable sizes, for use in churches, country houses, pubs, and homes wanting a touch of the unusual.

Pews seem to have got into the bloodstream of Christians over the past hundred years. Many a parent was glad of the way small children could be 'contained' in them, but most people have come to prefer the comfort and the lighter appearance of the chairs which were to take their place. Given the strong association of church interiors and pews, it is hardly surprising that long after they disappeared from St Nicholas in the summer of 1993, people reading the lesson still occasionally refer to a page number in the 'pew Bible'. It is strange to think that within a few years, most people under 25 won't even know what they looked like!

2: Life in exile

From now on, the weekly notice sheet would carry a large number on the top right hand side. The following Sunday it read 78, and the week after that, 77. No one needed an explanation. This was the number of weeks left before the church would return 'home'.

Through the generosity of the Headmaster of Sevenoaks School, morning services were held in the school's Aisher Hall. Its tiered lecture-theatre style was very convenient. And as the school is virtually opposite the church, and all the children's groups had been held there for some years, it was familiar ground.

Not everyone could fit into the Aisher Hall, so the morning service was held twice, at 9.30am and 11.00am. This meant splitting the church family, and carried the possibility of some people not seeing others for over a year. To offset the downside of the arrangement, coffee was served between services, and those who went to the second service were encouraged to arrive early enough to have coffee first. It was inevitable that families with young children should prefer the early service, but all children's groups ran twice, to maintain a mix across both services as far as possible. The double service arrangement was not ideal, but there was no way around it. In the back of some people's minds even then was the question of whether the morning service in the new 650-seater St Nicholas might ever have to be split, if the church grew significantly. The project was, after all, called *building* for the gospel.

On Sunday evenings, people crammed into the Parish Hall. Within a fortnight, Contact had commandeered the whole back row, from one end of the hall to the other. No one minded that, and people got the message fairly quickly. Up and down the country, it is quite common to sit in the same part of a church week by week, even month by month and year by year. It had been like that for some members of St Nick's. Contact got away with reserving its long back row, but given the arrangements in the hall, this just wasn't practicable for others. They found themselves sitting next to people they had not met before. As everyone was in the same boat, there was an atmosphere of greater openness. Those times are looked back on with a sense of affection.

Running a church on three sites brings big logistical problems to those on whose heads they fall. In this case the heads were those of Ian Dobbie as Project Director and Bernard Sharp as verger. For the church family generally, it was simply a case of remembering the time and venues of the services. Part of the public address system had to be carried from the Aisher Hall to the Parish Hall after the morning services, as it would be needed there in the evening, and then returned for the following morning. On site in the Aisher Hall, all the service books, and the lectern, and other 'portable' church furniture had to be packed away at mid-day each Sunday to transform the place back into a school hall.

Aware that on any given Sunday there might be visitors to a town parish church, Ian Dobbie arranged a rota of volunteers to stand outside the church and point them in the right direction. One such visitor was a charming Japanese lady. She was visiting London for the first time, and made the journey down to Sevenoaks one Sunday morning, specially to see the church. It wasn't its ancient foundation which had drawn her, nor had she heard about *B for the G*. But in the 1920s, a missionary called Elsie Baker had been sent out by St Nicholas to work in Osaka. Sometime during her 40 years in East Asia, she had 'planted' the seed of the gospel in this Japanese visitor's life, others had since 'watered' and God had given the growth. St Nick's has members in missionary work in nine countries now, and prays for a lasting impact from their ministry. This lady's visit was a wonderful reminder of the way we are linked with the worldwide Church, and of how one woman from a comfortable English parish can have an influence for Christ which will stand the test of time. This was all the more remarkable in view of the fact that Shinto-Buddhism is so much a part of Japanese culture and can often seem virtually impenetrable.

As the months progressed, and the numbers on the notice sheets came down, two parallel strands ran continuously through church life from week to week. On the one hand there was the ongoing pastoral ministry, which looked very much the same as it did at any time between Sundays. On the other hand, there was the constant presence of the work on site, and its related questions.

An unresolved question is finally answered

The future of the Parish Hall was still unresolved, and this was not straightforward because of its use by Campaigners. The situation made for polarised views, each borne out of genuine concern for the best way ahead. The fact that the PCC had on several occasions declared its commitment to preserve the Campaigners' work did not seem to allay fears.

Half way through the exile, the PCC circulated a consultation paper to the whole church family entitled 'The Last Lap'. It covered the financial needs still outstanding, and three possible ways forward: (i) to draw in new money from a church family which had already given so much; (ii) to trim the budget slightly, though this could create problems for the future. For example, if the new road leading from the back of the church car park were delayed, planning permission for it could conceivably be lost; (iii) to sell the Parish Hall to cover the needed costs. The document outlined the particular loss Campaigners would feel if they had to move to alternative accommodation.

No one doubted the vital and distinctive role played by Campaigners in the life of the church. The only question in the minds of the PCC was its need to meet in that particular hall. A considerable amount of effort had already gone into scouring the town for a suitable alternative venue. The Wildernesse Boys' School had been a possibility. It would have given enough space in halls and classrooms, but the Campaigner leaders felt, understandably, that being spread around the building would not work well, as cohesion would be lost. Use of the school would also have incurred considerable expense. This, however, would be offset by the loss of maintenance cost of the hall – currently eating into church funds.

Surely God would lead in this, as he had in everything else. Yet there seemed no obvious answer. The division of views was unhelpful, and was hindering Christian fellowship among some. Comments and questions came in letters, telephone calls, and in conversations with the church staff and with PCC members. The outcome of the next PCC meeting, at which a decision on the hall would be taken, was awaited with more than a little interest. This was set for 8.00pm on 3 July 1994.

That morning, Miles and Sara Thomson were reading in Proverbs 21, which opens with a strong affirmation of God's sovereignty: 'The King's heart is in the hands of the Lord; he directs it like a watercourse wherever he pleases.' Christians can sometimes let that certainty of his ultimate control become faint in their thinking. Here was another reminder that everything was in his hands. As the strategy document was discussed, it became clear that, in principle, the hall would no longer be needed. It was unanimously agreed that it should be sold. Such unanimity was a precious thing. The way ahead for Campaigners was still not clear, but the confident vote of the PCC reflected their reliance on a sovereign God.

the confident vote showed reliance on a sovereign God

Every church in the country which has moved forward in a project like this probably has a similar story to tell of understandable concern in relation to one group or another. To hear how each of those situations was resolved would be faith-building. In St Nicholas the dénouement was entirely unexpected, and surely an answer to people's prayers. An unexpected approach came from the minister of St John's United Reformed Church, asking if the Campaigners would like to meet in his building. This was close to the leaders' own home, and provided excellent hall space and a much better kitchen for use by those working for cookery badges. Yet again a solution had been found which was better than people would have hoped for or imagined.

Growth and loss

From week to week, growth was sometimes very easy to see. One Sunday there were 19 babies in the crèche. This was a record. The crèche helpers longed to have adequate accommodation such as the undercroft would provide.

Despite the demands of the three-site church, evangelism remained the priority. Sir Fred Catherwood, then MEP for Cambridgeshire, spoke at a supper party in the Parish Hall which drew over a hundred people – church members and their invited friends. Andrew Wingfield-Digby, former captain of the Dorset cricket team and founder of Christians in Sport, and

Alan Knott, former Kent and England wicket-keeper, were after-dinner speakers one evening at the Vine Cricket Pavilion. Each related the Christian faith to his personal life and his public responsibilities. Events like these were firmly in the church calendar, and the possibility of not arranging them because of other distractions was never entertained. Likewise the weekly meetings of Mum & Co for mothers and nannies, and the retired men's lunches, continued to draw those from beyond the church family. People who wanted to think further about the Christian faith could then come to Sunday services, or join study groups set up specially for that purpose.

As we have seen, the undercroft project never commanded support from everyone in the church family; some felt they were being pressurised to give money, in spite of all that was done to avert this; others felt their pastoral needs were not being met as the staff had too much else on their minds. With the best will in the world, some things were bound to be overlooked, and no one would have claimed otherwise.

Several of those who were not in favour of the project continued to worship at St Nicholas by relegating the matter, and not allowing it to come between them and others in the church. But from time to time Miles found himself talking with people who were unable to do this, and who had resolved to leave. As with those who had left before the exile, Miles always 'left the door open' so they could come back without any embarrassment once the undercroft was completed, if they wanted to.

One Sunday

It was impossible to divide what was happening on site from the ongoing life of the church. The parallel strands of pastoral ministry and *B for the G* can be typically described by one Sunday in October 1994. Unexpected news had arrived that week: the electricians working in the undercroft had gone into liquidation. With some 40 workmen on the site on most days, there was a great deal of interdependence among them. Often one group had to finish a job before another could move in and start work. It was vital that replacement electricians be found, very soon, and at the same cost. The matter was shared with the church family in the services, and they were asked to pray. Such setbacks could serve either to undermine confidence, or to redouble people's praying. By this stage, there was still a shortfall of £400,000. The next gift day was just three weeks ahead. So Paul Batchelor and Chris Webb once more presented the financial picture to the church family.

That afternoon the regular tea party for newcomers was held in the Parish Hall. As usual for this event, there were 20 or so people new to St Nicholas. Some were tentatively looking into the Christian faith; others had recently moved to Sevenoaks. Miles would show them slides of church life

people had to have undivided attention

and explain what went on during the week. To present a staff team preoccupied with the building fund would not be right. It would be a travesty of pastoral ministry. Whatever pressures the building work was bringing, people had to have undivided attention. Over and again the staff had found reassurance and help in their personal Bible reading to enable them to give that.

In the evening, Bob Marsden, the curate, preached from Luke's gospel on true discipleship. This was no plea for money. It was a plain exhortation from Christ himself to be serious about our priorities, if we call him Lord. Though money was needed for the undercroft, this was constantly and consistently regarded as of secondary importance to the biblical priorities of nurturing the life of Christ in people. To maintain integrity, the emphasis of the passage *itself* was to be taught. Bible passages were not used as a base on which to overlay an appeal for money.

More pledges – then the Barings news

The whole period of exile was one of looking ahead, and giving inevitably played a significant role in that. The fourth major Pledge Sunday arrived, to raise the balance required. The church once more looked to God for what was needed for all things come from him: there is no other primary source. Once again envelopes were placed in baskets as people came in, with pledges from some who had been giving since the beginning of the project, from others who had come in midstream, and from new people for whom this was their first opportunity to give. At 9.00pm Paul Batchelor rang the Rectory with the news that a further £85,000 had been covenanted, and £250,000 had been promised in interest-free loans. Giving rose to £97,000 by that Monday afternoon. Wonderful news!

Even 'money in the bank' was not completely safe, as nothing is in this world, and there were interesting moments caused by various external factors throughout the years. When the collapse of Barings Bank made world news on 3 March 1995, all its investors must have gone through an anxious few days. The Batchelors and others close to the finances of *B for the G* knew that this affected the church, as the Central Board of Finance of the Church of England, with whom St Nicholas funds were held, had money there on deposit. Barings' world-famous sale to the Dutch group, ING, for £1 on 6 March brought relief and thankfulness.

3: On site at St Nicholas

After they arrived on site, James Longley, one of the largest firms of construction engineers in the southeast, spent the rest of August preparing for work to begin. The Rectory garden soon housed portakabins for Gary Harper, the site manager, and for his men, and the war memorial in front of the church was taken down for safe-keeping. The residents in the immediate area were doubtless bracing themselves for a measure of inconvenience which would be inevitable.

The way we were

One of the terms on which the Diocesan Chancellor had granted permission for the project, was that archaeological research be allowed, and be paid for by the church. The PCC had accepted this. St Nicholas was a site of important historic interest, and there would be clues about Sevenoaks history, and wider English history, buried underneath the floor. It was hoped, however, that the archaeology would not drag on for a long time, as it cost money and curtailed some of the activities of the work force. The Oxford Archaeological Unit arrived in September under the sympathetic leadership of David Miles. To keep the costs to a minimum and to expedite the dig, volunteers from the church family, and from the town more widely, joined the team. No one knew the scale of the operation in advance, nor could anyone guess it. These volunteers, co-ordinated by Margaret Carpenter, brought their own coffee mugs with them, and for several hours a day brushed dirt off hundreds of skeletons for the specialists to analyse and record. Their help saved the project hundreds of pounds.

Archaeologists were on site for a total of 17 weeks, from early September right through to Christmas. One concern from St Nick's point of view was that this phase could take up a disproportionate amount of funding which had, after all, been given for forward-looking spiritual work, not for arcane research. Having said that, some findings could be of benefit for medical science: those, for example that threw light on social conditions in previous generations, and how they related to cause of death. Some skeletons were taken to London hospitals and others to the Oxford Archaeological Unit for detailed examination prior to reburial. All the findings were carefully noted for inclusion in the Unit's final report.

A previous re-ordering in Victorian times had created a charnel pit containing the remains of many of those who had been buried beneath the church. There had been some 500 burials there altogether, dating from the 12th century to the most recent in the 1840s. Twelve vaults were found, containing 70 lead coffins. There was also a foundry pit, where the church's bells were probably cast in early times.

Sevenoaks Library now houses a permanent display of trophies from the archaeological dig as part of its Sevenoaks Museum. These include a coin from the 12th century, fragments of painted glass and floor tiles from the 13th and 14th centuries, a 13th century brooch, and 17th century iron 'coffin furniture' (brackets and handles).

Safety on site

Constructing the undercroft was a complex operation with so many on site at the same time. Gary Harper, the overall manager, knew what he was taking on. The first thought he had on seeing the plans was that this would be the most difficult contract he had handled, and so it proved to be.

There were worrying moments, some known only to the work force. The church family was continually asked to pray, and to keep on praying, and not to presume on matters of safety. The feat itself – underpinning a medieval building – was unique in the world. One evening a friend from the Thomsons' previous parish in Harold Wood telephoned the Rectory. He said he had found it hard to sleep the night before, and had spent time praying for the undercroft. This occurred during the piling, and at a critical stage, although neither he nor the Thomsons realised that at the time.[1] Later, when an engineer came to say goodbye after the piling had been completed, he admitted he'd never been on a job with so many mechanical failures, adding that he himself had had three sleepless nights worrying whether the structure would collapse. The church staff felt relieved to have been protected from this worry, and thankful that they had heard about it only afterwards.

Once a fortnight, Robert Potter would chair a site meeting, at which he would always invite Ian Dobbie to open proceedings with prayer. For some of the work force chiefs, this was the first time they had prayed since their school assembly days. The prayer was more than a functional start to a business

there were two accidents to workmen on site

meeting on church premises. It was a public expression of dependence on God for the ongoing success of the work. At these meetings, the previous fortnight's progress was appraised, plans were laid for the coming two weeks, and any difficulties, actual or potential, were discussed. It was not unusual, for example, for two parties to want access to the same section of the site at the same time, to do jobs which needed to be tackled serially. Robert Potter was a skilled leader who drew everyone in with a view to finding a decision which would be widely accepted.

There were two accidents to workmen over the period of 'exile'. One man cut his thumb badly and had to be rushed to hospital for stitches. Two days later, the eight-year-old daughter of one of the churchwardens was inspecting progress at the site. Like many children of her age, she had a slightly morbid side to her nature, so when she heard about the accident, she went on her own investigative trail, tracing drips of blood from the church right down to the site office in the Rectory garden!

Then another workman had a trench close in on him, and he was suddenly buried up to his neck in sand while digging a drainage gully. It could have been very serious. The vibrations of the High Street traffic and of the machine tool he was using, together with the effect of heavy rainfall, had dislodged the metal props and steel sheets supporting the trench vertically. He was rescued and taken to hospital with severely pulled tendons. There was cause to keep on praying, and to be thankful to God for his protection.

Traffic chaos

Ian Dobbie and Gary Harper worked hard to keep any nuisance caused by the project down to a minimum, not least for the sake of the local residents. On two occasions, traffic was brought to a standstill, once rather amusingly (in retrospect!). Temporary traffic lights had been erected on the narrow High Street immediately outside the church while the undercroft drains were being integrated into the town drainage system. Miles and Sara noticed that lights had been left on in the church at the end of the working day, and assumed that the men had simply forgotten to turn them off. So Miles went across to rectify the matter. What he did not realise, however, was that the traffic lights had been hooked up to the church lights, which had been left on for that very reason! Completely unaware of the difficulties this action would cause right through to the next morning, he walked back to the Rectory.

Evening rush hours are one thing, but morning rush hours are quite another...

Evening rush hours are one thing, but morning rush hours are quite another...

At the beginning of the piling operation, a huge water tank had been installed at the front of the church, on the site of the war memorial, to allow for the 5,000 gallons of water per hour which were needed to drive the 72 piles into the ground. In mid February 1994 this operation was complete, and the tank could be removed. A crane was due to arrive early one morning to lift the tank away. The job needed to be done early, or it would cause havoc for the rush hour traffic as soon as it started to flow. Seven o'clock came and went. By half past seven there was still no sign of the crane, and Ian knew there would be a serious problem for people driving to work. It had been a bad winter's night, which slowed the progress of the truck bringing the crane, and it was eight o'clock by the time it eventually arrived. There was nothing Ian could do apart from rely on the good nature of those driving to work, and the understanding of their bosses when they arrived late. By the time traffic was moving again, there were tailbacks from the White Hart to Riverhead – one and a half miles in both directions – some very irate drivers, and a cause for profuse apologies.

One massive pile of dirt (and handling discouragement)

A total of some 3,500 cubic metres of soil, sand and rubble were removed from beneath the church floor over the period, and diggers emptied their loads into the Rectory garden. Each week, three 32-ton wagons would arrive to load up this landfill, and drive it over to the borrow pit in Edenbridge, ten miles away. They repeated this process up to six times in that day, to clear the garden for the next week's diggings.

Access and egress could be gained only via Rectory Lane, as there was no other road off the site. But its narrowness, and its junction with the narrow High Street so near a double bend, did not provide ideal conditions for the drivers. Given that the church was surrounded by homes on each side, and that the site itself was such a confined space for its teams of workmen, Gary Harper's careful co-ordination worked extremely well, and the general good humour of the local residents made for a largely problem-free time.

The original plan of 78 weeks was not to be. The finishing date was shunted back on three or four occasions, to Easter, to April, to May, and finally to June 1995. Prices for work were slowly creeping up, and it was sometimes hard to keep believing in the providence of God as each delay inevitably brought another thud of disappointment. Back in 1992, while permission for the project was still uncertain, Miles had preached on the story of Joseph from Genesis, and his need for patience when he was in prison, wrongfully accused of trying to seduce Potiphar's wife. Miles had extrapolated from this the way Christians should handle themselves, with God's help, when they were 'up against it' in life. It had been a timely lesson for everyone. The Thomsons, Ian Dobbie and the wardens were the most vulnerable to discouragement as delays occurred, and they set the tone for the church family by their own reactions.

The hole and the time capsule

As soon as there was a hole which was deep enough to be worth looking at, the church was open to the public for an hour on the second Saturday of each month. This gave any townspeople with an interest the chance to see what was happening, to ask questions, and to follow the progress of the undercroft's construction, as 80 tons of concrete gradually formed the new undercroft floor. These mornings drew only a few, but this gesture of goodwill seemed to be appreciated, and the local press picked up news of the openings on several occasions.

Every now and again the church was opened on a Sunday morning after each of the services. This meant members of the church family could walk over from Sevenoaks School to follow progress.

As work began on the floor of the church, it was felt appropriate that a time capsule be buried beneath the chancel. What would best encapsulate the project: its purpose, its location, its timing? The following articles were chosen, and packed into an airtight plastic box: the *Sevenoaks Chronicle* on micofilm; a New Testament; a *B for the G* mug and video; a pound coin; a first class postage stamp; a Lady Boswell's School sweatshirt; a copy of the current James Longley's newsletter, and the Sarum Partnership logo.

Chapter 8

Moving back 'home'

Form must follow function. Any architect knows that. Careful attention had been paid throughout the undercroft's design stages to the way the rooms would be used. Now it was time to plan for making that happen. Terry Boxall, a retired surgeon, was asked by the PCC to look at possible uses of the undercroft during the week, so the facilities did truly *facilitate* 'building for the gospel'. He consulted widely within the church family, and visited churches in Bristol, Winchester and Guildford, as well as in nearby Tonbridge, to see what could be learned from the way others did things. He presented a report on his findings to the PCC.

The Annual Church Meeting gave just the right setting for the church family to discuss possible new uses of the extra space. The perfect balance was to be found in exploiting every way the building could be used by those outside the church, while not inhibiting its use by church groups.

Out of Terry's report grew plans for the bookshop and coffee shop, which were opened straight away in the summer of 1995. It was clear that extra staff would be needed to run these, perhaps partly salaried and partly made up of volunteers. Many town uses would naturally 'grow' once the premises were opened and available, and one could only speculate on the extent or range of that. However it was important to listen to, and engage with, dreams and ideas from the church family early on. Now alongside the regular use made by church groups, there are specialist lectures, concerts and children's activities run by townspeople for whom the undercroft or the newly re-ordered church, with its adjacent car park, is ideal.

Naming the rooms

There were to be four halls in the undercroft, and they needed names. One could refer to 'the crèche' on a Sunday, but it would be put to several uses during the week; other rooms likewise. Some people suggested the names be linked with Knole House. It would have made sense, and there was a

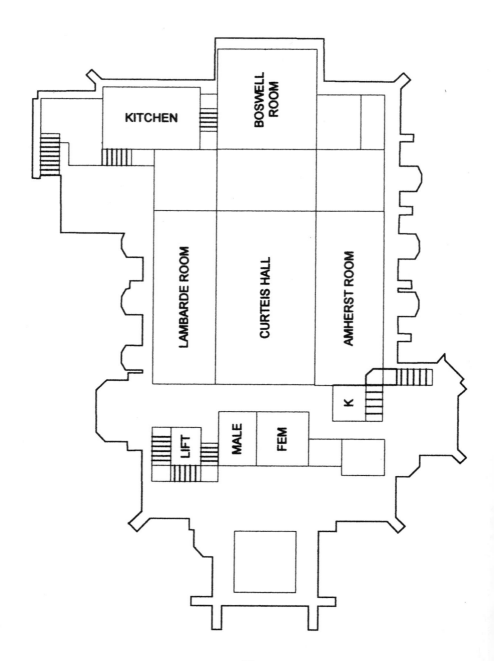

good deal of sympathy for that line of thought. Others suggested they be named after the Reformers: either the great figureheads like John Calvin, Martin Luther, John Wyclif or Nicholas Ridley, or the lesser-known martyrs in the southeast of England. (A memorial to those from Kent and Sussex who died in 1555 under the despotic Queen Mary stands above the town of Lewes.) Again, the idea gained much support. However, though St Nick's has looked back with thankfulness to God for the Reformation martyrs who gave their lives for the cause of truth, it had no direct link historically with the Reformation. In the end it was decided to name the rooms after prominent Sennockians who had been buried beneath the church. The undercroft had been built to serve Sevenoaks town, so it was felt that marking local history would be most fitting. They are, then:

The Boswell Room. This is named after Lady Margaret Boswell, founder of the primary school which bears her name. She died in 1692, leaving endowments for education locally, and for scholarships to Jesus College, Cambridge. There is a striking, sculptured memorial to her life and her achievements on the wall of the north aisle in the church.

The Curteis Hall. Five generations of the Curteis family held office as Rectors of Sevenoaks for a total of 190 years, with only two short breaks. Revd Thomas Curteis, the last in the line, oversaw major internal work and removed galleries to make the church interior brighter. His grandfather, Dr Thomas Curteis, had the church bells recast, so the old peal of six bells became the new peal of eight; he also amalgamated the offices of rector and vicar.

The Lambarde Room. The Lambardes or Lambards were a distinguished and influential local family over several generations. John Lambarde was a sheriff of London in the reign of Elizabeth I. His son, William, was Keeper of the Rolls of the Tower and author in 1570 of *A Perambulation of Kent*, subtitled 'conteining the description, hystorie, and customes of that shire'. This was the first county history of its kind.

The Amherst Room. In 1760, Jeffrey Amherst led the armies which conquered Canada. This was achieved by converging three British armies in a complex operation with few equals in military history. On returning to Britain he was made a Field Marshal and Commander-in-Chief of the British Army. To mark this success in his home town, he built a new family

Photos (right) by the kindness of Alex Watson Sevenoaks Chronicle

seat, calling it Montreal, and the Montreal Park estate commemorates this.

The story of the organ

Fifteen years earlier, in a partial re-ordering of the church, the pipe organ had been replaced by an electronic instrument. The pipe organ itself had been both enlarged and modified on so many occasions that it could no longer be said to represent the work of any one builder; and shoe-horned, as it was, into the northeast corner of the chancel, it was never heard to best effect. Purists can be disparaging about electronic substitutes, but Peter Young, the organist, described the change in positive vein: 'The electronic organ had the merit of speaking out directly into the body of the nave, and it greatly enhanced the singing,' he said. 'But the best acoustic performance was in the end unachievable. We would never have received a Faculty for the ideal positioning of the speaker cabinets. This illustrates the tensions between aesthetics and practicability.'

In re-ordering for *B for the G*, it was agreed that there be as little fixed furniture as possible in the church, for the sake of maximum flexibility, and this applied to the organ console, too. The original organ, dating back to 1798, had been installed in the gallery at the west end of the church, blocking much of the light from its high window. The possibility of a new pipe organ was explored, but in the end it was agreed to opt for an electronic replacement, largely on grounds of finance. With the decision to reinstate a gallery under the tower, it was agreed that the new organ console be placed there, and that the choir, too, move to this location. The new organ, from the Bradford Computing Organ Company, has speakers at the east end (in the old pipe organ case), and high up at the west end, under the roof of the gallery. A simple switching system makes it possible for the organ to speak from the east or west ends only, or from both simultaneously. 'This has worked very well,' says Peter, 'and the re-positioning of the choir on the gallery has been, chorally speaking, pure gain.'

Getting it right

Interior décor is conspicuous when it is not appropriate, and a joy to the eye when it is 'just right'. If designers choose the colour of the year,

St Nicholas Campaigners march to church for a parade service

whether that is pink, green or purple, it will very soon look dated, lovely though it may seem at the time. Margaret Potter had worked with her husband on several major projects, and had brought her aesthetic judgment to churches and cathedrals. She met with Jenny Jennings and her *'ambience* team', and together they discussed the colours of the chairs and carpet for the church and for the undercroft. After visits to several churches and to the bewilderingly-huge Christian Resources Exhibition at Sandown Park, they chose the same chairs as are used in Chelmsford Cathedral. Their pale terracotta fabric catches the sun, and adds a lightness to the church in a decidedly pleasing way. The carpet is an unobtrusive pale brown.

Each of the chairs in the chancel was to have an embroidered kneeler, and there were to be long cushions extending right round the steps at the communion rail. These would depict local themes of Knole House, Knole Park and its deer, the Vine Cricket Club, Sevenoaks School,

The west door, with the Lord's final command and promise, before he ascended to heaven

Lady Boswell's School, and the seven acorns of Sevenoaks town. The designers, Angela Dewar and Gisela Banbury, trained Sarah Amott in how to embroider the cushions, and she in turn trained up a team to work on them over the next few years. It was to be a labour of love.[1]

continuity with the past is a value not to be lost

Continuity with the past is a value not to be lost. In 1985 when it looked as if a new integrated church building might be some way away, the PCC had decided to brighten up the Parish Hall as well as it could be done. The usual self-help method was used, with a small gang of volunteer painters. One church member saw some soft material at a good price while on holiday in south Germany, and made an on-the-spot decision to buy it for curtains. These were hung on each side of the hall's high windows, and around the stage. And new chairs were purchased for the upstairs lounge used by Contact. Ruby Walters, a longstanding member of the church, now took those curtains and used the material to cover all those new chairs, for use in the undercroft. Again, here was a labour of love.

The church needed a new communion table. In keeping with evangelical theology, it would be placed much further forward than previously. Jonathan Woodrow, a furniture maker who was an old boy of Sevenoaks School, and a member of St Nicholas, was commissioned for the task. The table he made is of light oak, and stands six and a half feet long. Its design is simple, in the Reformed tradition.

Getting it wrong!

One of the last jobs to be done in the church before the work was completed was to hang the west end glass doors, inscribed: 'Go into all the world and make disciples, and surely I am with you always, to the very end of the age'. This was the Lord's final command and promise before he ascended to heaven. The double doors stand three feet inside an outer set of doors, and have the inscription written across them. It made sense to the fitters to hang them so that anyone coming in from outside could read them. One saw their logic. However, Miles arrived as this was happening, and was able to correct the error. The words, as he explained, are an exhortation to Christians to go out into Sevenoaks and to the world beyond, to make disciples. So they are intended to be read by people as they *leave* the church building, not as they enter it.

The opening week

On Sunday, 18 June, 1995, the evening service in the Parish Hall closed with the first verse of the hymn which had taken the church family out of St Nicholas almost two years earlier: 'How good is the God we adore!' Since then, there had been two momentous years in which to learn more of his goodness. Again, everyone moved to the new venue for the second verse, so it was the reverse operation of what had happened before. The building was not yet handed back, so it was not possible to go in, but people gathered outside the west door. Miles hesitated as he was about to announce the second verse. Were 'the Dorothys' there yet? Doris Colgate's friends Dorothy Badman and Dorothy Corke walked a little more slowly than others, and everyone needed to be together for this. The two Dorothys, who have since both died, were typical of a large band of elderly people who had been in St Nick's for decades. Faced with change, they did not react against it, but weighed the arguments. Not only were they accepting of it, but they welcomed it.

The church was jammed full for the opening service three days later. The two previous rectors and their wives, Ken and Dorothy Prior and Eric and Edith McLellan, sent their greetings. In the truest sense, the undercroft was a gift from God. On a human level, it was the culmination of prayer, faith, sacrificial giving and sheer hard work – not only for the previous five years, but stretching back for 30 years. David Jackman, Director of the Cornhill Training Course, was the guest preacher, and Bishop Ken Barham of Rwanda, a former St Nicholas curate, represented the Bishop of Rochester.

The choir, from their new position in the gallery at the west end of the church, sang the verses from Paul's letter to the Ephesians which expressed that 'very great promise' to which Michael Baughen had referred six years earlier. Knowing how this promise had sustained Miles, Ian and the building committee throughout the long process, Peter Young wrote a special setting of it for the occasion (see Appendix 1). Those verses are now engraved on a plaque half way down the stairs to the undercroft:

> Now to him who is able to do immeasurably more than all we ask or imagine, according to his power that is at work within us, to him be glory in the church and in Christ Jesus throughout all generations, for ever and ever, Amen.

The church prayer diary, enabling members of St Nick's to pray for one another and for God's work more widely, includes a verse or two of Scripture for each day, and these verses roll on unchanged from year to year. Earlier that week Miles had stolen a march on the reading for the day of the opening service. It was Ephesians 3:20,21 – the same verses. A wonderful confirmation of God's timing.

David Jackman preached from Peter's first letter to the early Jewish Christians. In 1 Peter 2, the apostle describes Jesus Christ as the 'cornerstone' of a building, and Christians as being 'living stones' who are built into a spiritual house. He drew attention to the three key verbs in the passage: *come* to him, *believe* in him, *obey* him. In re-dedicating the building, there was

come to him, believe in him, obey him

an opportunity to re-dedicate our lives to God – our time, energy, skills and resources – as 'spiritual sacrifices'. In these ways, St Nick's would bring glory to Christ, not only in Sevenoaks, but in the whole world.

Yet again there was an opportunity to give money – not for St Nicholas, but for building projects in three other countries with which the church had links: Rwanda, so appallingly riven by its recent violence, now rebuilding its churches; and Tanzania and Benin.

The following week was full of parties. Everyone in the parish was invited to coffee in the undercroft on one or another evening, and taken on a tour of the refurbished church. They were shown slides of the whole process - beginning, middle and end - and after all the reports in the *Sevenoaks Chronicle*, now had a chance to see what had been done for themselves. Lady Boswell's classes also came up, one a day, to be shown around.

The next Saturday at 8.00am a group met to pray, in the undercroft. So many prayers had been heard for those extra rooms, stretching over thirty years – and they were now a reality. It was, fittingly, Tony Wilmot's birthday.

All the men who had worked on the site were invited to bring their families for lunch that day. Few ever saw the 'end product' of their labours since once their own skills were no longer necessary, they moved on to other jobs. This was therefore a particularly memorable day for them. Miles showed his slides, so that their families could get a feel for how great a project it had been. And then, in the bright church the men had worked to re-create, everyone sang a hymn together, familiar from schooldays for most, if not all. After sharing in a short prayer of thanks for the skills God had given them to complete the task with such care, Miles gave a short talk, and then passed everyone a copy of the booklet *New Beginnings* by Richard Bewes to take home.

Celebration Praise

Richard Bewes had succeeded Michael Baughen as Rector of All Souls, Langham Place. He came down to St Nicholas to preach at the evening service the next day, and the All Souls Orchestra, led by Noel Tredinnick, joined forces with the St Nick's musicians for the occasion. The Waldegrave Hall underneath All Souls had been an inspiration to St Nick's at the outset. Bishop Michael, who had led that church through its delicate and costly building project in the 1970s, had brought a warm and enthusiastic exhortation to move out in faith six years earlier. Who better to lead the Celebration Praise that evening than his successor?

St Nicholas had achieved its goal. And it was some achievement! On that summer's evening, with the light streaming through the windows, the church almost shone. There was every reason to feel pleased, and there were also all the subtle dangers of self-congratulation. Four days earlier the new building had been formally opened, with many visitors and local dignitaries there for the occasion. Now the church family was back home on its own, and the visitors had gone. Richard Bewes turned to the New Testament, and the final chapter of Paul's letter to the Galatians.

> May I never boast, except in the cross of our Lord Jesus Christ, through which the world has been crucified to me and I to the world.

The words went to the heart of the gospel, with all its paradoxes of death and life, joy and pain. For all that had been achieved in human terms – by those who planned, those who gave money, and those who brought practical skills to the project – the undercroft was nothing to boast about. But the cross of Christ was everything to boast about. It was, he said, 'the epicentre of the Christian faith' and 'the great interpreter of life'. By it, and only by it, could values be measured; it was 'the definer of all choices'.

the cross is 'the great interpreter of life'

Handel's *Hallelujah Chorus* brought everyone to their feet. An ancient building had been altered for the 21st century; a medieval church for post-modernity. But here was the cross on which Christ had died: the cross which divided time in half; and the King of kings and Lord of lords, who would reign for ever and ever.

PART II

Chapter 9

Building for the gospel

B *for the G* had, in a sense, been going on in St Nick's long before the building project started, and it will always be part of the church's life. Paul wrote to the Corinthian Christians about building for the gospel in their own lives:

> By the grace God has given me, I laid a foundation as an expert builder, and someone else is building on it. But each one should be careful how he builds. For no one can lay any foundation other than the one already laid, which is Jesus Christ. If any man builds on this foundation using gold, silver, costly stones, wood, hay or straw, his work will be shown for what it is, because the Day will bring it to light. It will be revealed with fire, and the fire will test the quality of each man's work. If what he has built survives, he will receive his reward. If it is burned up, he will suffer loss; he himself will be saved, but only as one escaping through the flames.
> (I Corinthians 3:10-15)

Leaders in Climbers, Explorers, Centrepoint, Contact and Campaigners are all the time 'building' in the lives of their members; preachers and homegroup leaders are 'building' in the lives of the adults. God has given special gifts to some in the church so that – together and individually – the whole church family can be built up. In his letter to the Christians in Ephesus, Paul was clear about his aim: '...until we all reach unity in the faith and in the knowledge of the Son of God and become mature, attaining to the whole measure of the fulness of Christ' (Ephesians 4:12,13). This is the essence of Christian ministry.

B for the G in **Contact**

The upper years of school are a critical stage in shaping values and setting patterns for life, and the St Nick's curate treats Contact as his first priority.

Contact members meet in groups around the town for Bible study on a Friday night, as well as getting together after the evening service on a Sunday. In term time, several leaders meet weekly with two or three

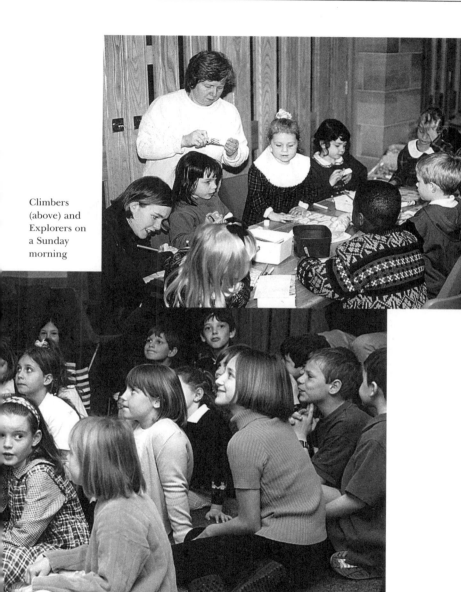

Climbers (above) and Explorers on a Sunday morning

The annual Contact houseparty: evidently serious stuff

Contact members to form a 'prayer triplet'. Here they talk through what's going on at school, and in life more generally, and they pray for their friends. This is all part of the many-sided process of preparing, equipping and training them for the part they can play in God's wider church: in the student world, in their families, in their careers. Not a few have entered the pastoral ministry, or become cross-cultural missionaries.

B for the G beyond the parish boundaries

Contact is one of the more visible expressions of *B for the G*. But through teaching and influencing in the life of the whole church family, the orbit of St Nicholas goes far beyond its parish boundaries. 'We are God's fellow workers' (1 Corinthians 3:9) and must 'build well' not only in our own lives, but in the lives of those around us. When Tony Wilmot urged the church to look for 'heaven's dividends', he was surely referring to the fruit of this work.

Church life can sometimes be perceived by its members simply in terms of 'us and God'. The call to be salt and light in society, and to bring the good news of the gospel to friends, neighbours and colleagues, can slip off the edge of Christian thinking. The whole earth belongs to God, and Christians are in a sense re-claiming it for him. This applies in different ways to teachers, businessmen, medics and so forth, and everyone needs help in learning how to apply biblical principles in their work. A local church will not have specialists in all these areas, but leaders can encourage the whole church family to work at 'thinking Christianly', and point people in the right direction for stimulus and guidance.[1]

Through praying, we can also 'build for the gospel' in the lives of people we have never met. St Nicholas missionaries are engaged in a wide range of activities: we have already met one couple who produce literature for the people of Ethiopia; another couple pastors a small church in Argentina; a young woman works with students in Russia; others are in North America, Africa, Asia and Europe, or in the student world of our own country. Several work in the UK offices of overseas missions. Whether on the 'front-line' or in the 'back room' they are all serving Christ's Church around the world. And as St Nick's members get behind them in prayer, the whole church is 'building for the gospel' on university campuses, in villages and small towns, and in the world's megacities, sometimes close by, sometimes thousands of miles away.

Two former members of Contact are now engaged in very different ministries in our own country. We focus first on an urban priority area in Liverpool, and then on the work of the Jubilee Centre.

B for the G in Toxteth

David Gavin was a member of Contact in the late 1970s and early 1980s. Since 1995, he has been vicar of St Cleopas, in Toxteth, Liverpool where the gradual demise of the Merseyside docks since the war has led to a steady and unrelenting rise in unemployment, with all its associated problems. National news focused on this part of Liverpool in 1981 when it, like other parts of the country facing a similar state of depression, became the scene of rioting.

Television sitcoms portray Liverpudlians as tough survivors. They can come through anything by drawing on natural wit and a sense of humour passed on through the genes, or caught by osmosis. The Boswell family of *Bread* fame were survivors. Their house is in the parish of St Cleopas, so these streets became known to millions of viewers in the late 1980s.

Almost everything about St Cleopas is different from St Nick's. Almost everything about Toxteth is different from Sevenoaks. David's church members tend to live within a mile of the church. Many are unemployed, or earn very little in temporary or casual employment. Many members of St Nick's work in the City, or elsewhere in London, and business trips can take them away for 80-100 nights a year or more, either in the UK or overseas; this has an inevitable knock-on effect in terms of church life as well as family life. Yet for all the differences in circumstances and in routines and their effects on family life, the two churches have much in common. Each is made up of people who want to worship God and want to know him better; people rubbing shoulders with colleagues and neighbours during the week who follow some other faith, or have no faith at all. One does not want to minimize the differences. But the similarities are profound.

almost everything about St Cleopas is different from St Nick's, but the similarities are profound

David's parents and his brother and family still worship at St Nick's, and David and Jan have followed the undercroft story with more than a little interest. They saw how God worked in people's thinking to change attitudes, and how opposition to the extension schemes proved to be God's means of creating a far better way forward. They saw how God moved the hearts of church members to give, and to keep on giving. Could there be a miracle like that in Toxteth?

Cleo's, as it is known locally, would have needed radical repair work to maintain its present hall. But that building is far from adequate, and the

David Gavin's story

David grew up in Mount Harry Road, Sevenoaks. At 15, life took a new turn, at first through the influence of a friend from Sevenoaks School, Andrew Hodder-Williams. Andrew was a member of Contact, and David started to go along there with him on a Friday night. David's sister was already part of the group. Here was a chance to get to know some other Christians, and to find out what they believed. That summer term, in 1979, he became a Christian.

In August, Donald Allister arrived at St Nick's as a curate and began a three-year doctrine course for Contact, one Friday a month. It was a complete systematic theology in 45-minute bytes and around 60-70 would crowd into the Parish Hall for it.

David took a gap year to teach English and maths in Uttar Pradesh with a schoolfriend, who was an atheist. On their first Sunday, the local church leader invited them both to preach, simply because they were English! David's friend declined as a matter of integrity. David accepted, mainly because he had been so disappointed by the lack of biblical content in Sunday sermons. At 18 this was a big step.

Not having his Contact friends around, David became much more dependent on God, and on his personal Bible study and prayer. At the end of the six months, the two returned to Britain. His friend now described himself as agnostic. It was a move in the right direction!

At Birmingham University, David became evangelism secretary in the Christian Union. In his final year, he heard from Andrew Hodder-Williams that Donald Allister, by then in Birkenhead, needed a youth worker. Drawn by the idea of getting good training in this area, he went to Birkenhead for one year after he graduated – and stayed there for three.

David chose Cranmer Hall, Durham, for theological training as the college owned a flat in Gateshead where students could live. This was a world away from Sevenoaks, and from academia, and he loved the mix it gave of practical and pastoral ministry alongside his studies.

Four years followed in a curacy at St Peter Parr, St Helen's, under the leadership of David Thompson. Then in 1995 he and his wife, Jan, moved to Toxteth. They have two children.

money would not be well invested in simply keeping it up. So in 1998 the Church moved out – in faith – and launched an appeal for a new St Cleopas Church and Family Centre. There will be some funding from national trusts, but Cleo's members and friends have committed themselves to finding £50,000 themselves. No one thinks it will be easy. With unemployment, and a high proportion of single parent families, all giving will be sacrificial. But the time is ripe; the church is growing, and with several blocks of nearby post-war flats now being demolished, it would be possible to move to a better site. They have plans for parenting classes and for support groups for carers, and those who are separated or divorced. They want to hold special services and other activities for those with learning disabilities, and to provide a meeting place for the elderly and for the young people. The facilities would also be used to create a safe meeting place in which children from broken families could meet absentee or estranged parents. All these inroads into the community would be a natural part of the church's evangelism.

This former member of Contact is reflecting the same values, and the same aspirations, praying to the same God for the sake of the same gospel.

B for the G in society

The Jubilee Centre is in Cambridge. It began in a back room of Michael Schluter's home in 1983, and had barely moved to its own offices in 1986 when the Keep Sunday Special campaign brought it into the media limelight.

The motivation behind its initiatives is simply that the Bible makes sense, and biblical values and priorities are good for people personally and for society. For example Sunday trading would deny working parents a guaranteed day at home once a week with their children. In offering Sunday overtime rates, it would undermine the value of that time. It would also undermine the pattern of work and rest set by God at creation. The Sabbath was, after all, made 'for man' (Mark 2:27,28), and not just for Christians.

If God is the creator, his values pertain to everyone, in a pluralistic society, as much as in a Christian community. The raison d'être of the Jubilee Centre is to bring Christian values into the arena of public policy in

Michael Schluter's story

The Schluter family moved to Sevenoaks when Michael was six months old. He was the third of four children. Wanting them to learn about God, his parents sent all of them to St Nicholas Sunday school. One Sunday afternoon the curate, Dick Lucas, found himself praying for the family, and he went down to visit them at their home in St George's Road. In due course the parents came to realize their church allegiance was mere formality, and that they did not know God for themselves. Michael was then six.

Two people were to have a profound influence on Michael Schluter as a boy. His Sunday school leader, Kath Arnold, a retired missionary, was one of them. She urged him to learn whole chapters of the Bible by heart, and he did this on the bus journey to Tonbridge School. When he was 14, she drew him into Sunday school teaching, and taught him the principles of how to marshal his material and how to present it. This training formed the foundation of his later public speaking. The second person was the curate, Hugh Sylvester, who ran Contact. 'He was a sharp thinker,' Michael remembers, 'and he was fun.'

Michael's father ran an international coffee business based in the City. Soon after becoming a Christian, he began meeting with four other City businessmen to pray for a Christian witness in the square mile. After five years, St Helen's in Bishopsgate fell vacant, and they persuaded the Bishop to put Dick Lucas into it. Dick Lucas's ministry there was to last until 1998 and, under God, to prove profoundly influential.

Michael read economics at Durham University, and like so many former Contact members, held leadership roles in the Christian Union as an undergraduate. Before going on to gain a PhD at Cornell University in the States, he spent a year in Uganda, working with Scripture Union. When his PhD was completed, he went to work in Kenya, and there met Roy Clements, now of the Fitzroy Trust, who was then pastor of Nairobi Baptist Church.

At first Michael was in the family business, then he moved to the World Bank, and on to the International Food Policy Research Institute. During that time, he and Roy explored ways of applying biblical principles to secular issues.

In 1982 he moved back to Britain, sensing God's call to find ways of bringing Christian values into secular public life. The Jubilee Centre grew from here.

areas like housing, education, employment and healthcare and to demonstrate their universality. It does this through initiatives and campaigns which are not confined to Christians, but which are based on Christian values. Its main arm in public life is the Relationships Foundation.

Relationships, says Michael, are the foundation of everything. 'We live in a society where even to speak to a small child in the street arouses suspicion. A society where many have to work a 12-hour day or suffer the risk of losing their job, regardless of how those at home are neglected. A society where elderly people often feel isolated as they are afraid to set foot outside their own home and where few, if any, take time to visit them...' The reasons for the current breakdown in relationships are complex, and the Jubilee Centre has no panacea to put past wrongs right. However it is working now to stop this breakdown from becoming worse, and to stop public policymakers from setting patterns which would cause a further downward trend in family values.

relationships are the foundation of everything

Unemployment in some city areas is very high, and can bring with it low self-esteem and isolation, as well as strained finances. An initiative in Sheffield, launched in 1999, aims to address this head on. The *Sheffield Employment Bond* is, in one sense, like any other investment bond. The investor puts in money and withdraws it at the end of an agreed period. In this case that period is five years. The capital has been worked hard. However, the interest is not added to the investor's account. It has been used to create employment by training unemployed people; by providing loans for entrepreneurs who want to start their own small businesses; by encouraging community enterprises; by enabling the North British Housing Association to build more new homes. This is a jointly owned enterprise with a network of key agencies. In some areas of this city, one fifth of the eligible workforce is without a job; over half the city's children are growing up in families with no wage earner. Sheffield is 'a great city'; the aim is to give it 'a future to work for'.

The Jubilee Centre has also worked for peace and reconciliation in South Africa and Rwanda. The African work, known as the Newick Park Initiative (named after Lord Brentford's home in Sussex where the first discussions were held), is staffed and financed separately from the UK work. However they share a common basis, for both were born out of a concern for Christ's name to be honoured, and for his priorities to be lived out in public life, and not just in the church and in the home.

New plant, new opportunities

For St Nick's the building was never to be an end in itself, and even before the undercroft was opened, the PCC was looking hard at how to make the premises most effective. They wanted to see an authentic Christianity lived out in the town, and Christ's name being honoured in people's lives, motives, aspirations and careers. As a church, much had been given to us, and much would be required of us. Christ's command, etched on the west door, to 'Go into all the world and make disciples' is a constant reminder of our mandate.

What a church 'does' springs from its identity. Church isn't just a place we 'go to on Sundays'. Christ's Church is a body of people right round the world to which all Christians belong. And in the most complete sense, it also includes those who have died, and gone to be with him in heaven. The Church is a living, growing, worshipping community of people who love God. That is far, far more than a building.

John Stott's Afterword looks at the nature of the church in contemporary life, by going to the primary source on the matter, namely the Bible itself. The original plan given to the early Christians has not been superseded.

The art of belonging

The emphasis on church as people is brought out by the Lord Jesus, and by Paul. As fellow Christians, we belong to each other, and our faith is a corporate faith. We are told to encourage one another, counsel one another, love one another, and bear one another's burdens. It may seem trivial to move from exhortations like that to the benefits of talking over coffee after the Sunday services, but in a truly practical and down-to-earth way, the undercroft has helped the congregation to be built into a 'church family'. Newcomers can be welcomed there, new friendships can start, and existing friendships can grow. As Christians we are part of the Body of Christ. We need each other. We support each other.

Jurassic Park and post-modernity

If we have something worth saying, it will, by its nature, be culturally relevant, but it must also be communicated in a culturally relevant way. St Nicholas stands in a home counties town which is largely very comfortable, and this fact influenced the planning of the undercroft. It was to be designed and finished in the local 'idiom' to reflect the cultural relevance of the church.

In the realm of ideas, this 'cultural relevance' also applies to the prevailing mindset of the day. Christians do not adopt that mindset – though they may carry more of its underlying values than they realize – but they *do* operate within it. The Christian gospel must demonstrate that it holds water, that it has integrity, that it is for the academic and for the non-academic.

In what is now widely known as our 'postmodern society' we must work hard at helping one another to learn, love and obey Scripture. We have moved a long way since the 1960s in attitudes to authority, and Christians can easily lose a sense of Scripture being their authority – their authority on what is true, and on how to behave. The idea of 'truth' has been completely devalued in our highly-individualistic popular culture, as is summed up in the Manic Street Preachers' line 'This is my truth, tell me yours.' To Joe Public, it might seem quaint to think of the Bible as our authority for what to believe, and for how to live – here and now. He may say Jurassic Park is the best place for preachers.

Roy Clements of the Fitzroy Trust wrote a powerful apologetic for the place of preaching in today's western world, in which he looked at the influence of modern writers on the way we now tend to view all objective data.[2] The drift, he says, is towards subjective interpretations of everything. We prefer images to words, we rate our feelings more highly than concepts, and we trust intuition more than logic. The impact of these changes on how people view truth has been profound. He goes on:

The art of belonging

The Christian faith is a corporate faith and the Lord Jesus, the apostle Paul, and other New Testament writers reflect this in their teaching. The following list is not exhaustive:

MARK 9:50 Be at peace with each other

JOHN 13:34 A new command I give to you: Love one another

ROMANS 1:11,12 I long to see you... that you and I may be mutually encouraged by each other's faith

ROMANS 12:10 Be devoted to one another in brotherly love. Honour one another above yourselves

ROMANS 12:16 Live in harmony with one another

ROMANS 13:8 Let no debt remain outstanding, except the continuing debt to love one another

ROMANS 15:7 Accept one another, just as Christ accepted you

GALATIANS 6:2 Carry each other's burdens, and in this way you will fulfil the law of Christ

EPHESIANS 4:32 Be kind and compassionate to one another, forgiving each other, just as in Christ God forgave you

PHILIPPIANS 2:1-4 If you have any encouragement in being united with Christ ... each of you should look not only to your own interests, but to the interests of others

COLOSSIANS 3:16 Let the Word of Christ dwell in you richly as you teach and admonish one another with all wisdom

HEBREWS 3:13 Encourage one another daily, as long as it is called Today

HEBREWS 10: 24,25 Let us consider how we may spur one another on towards love and good deeds. Let us not give up meeting together, as some are in the habit of doing, but let us encourage one another

1 PETER 4:8,9 Above all, love each other deeply, because love covers over a multitude of sins. Offer hospitality to one another... Each one should use whatever gift he has received to serve others

Truth is increasingly regarded as something self-manufactured and provisional. Post-modernity rejects [all ideas of an over-arching plan for the universe], and offers instead the philosophical equivalent of Legoland, in which everyone is free to gather whatever pieces they like and build them into their own do-it-yourself Disneytruth to play with.

Disneytruth is far more palatable than true truth. And a Disney authority figure easier to cope with than the Lord God. Choosing what we want to believe and sticking those pieces together without any reference to 'the God who is there' can be a very attractive way of living, in this world. Whether we articulate it like that or not, it is how most people in Sevenoaks, and Toxteth, do live.

Disneytruth is far more palatable than true truth

But as a church family, we must express our different values, and 'live out' our commitment to what the apostle Paul called 'the most excellent way'. If the manner in which we conduct ourselves in business, or socially, is at odds with our Christian profession, then that will always have a negative value for the gospel. Christian lives must be infused with spiritual values. And, as salt and light in society, Christians must be concerned for public policy and for the way it bears on others.

A casual observer would be forgiven for thinking Christianity out of place in the postmodern world: superseded; redundant. A more reflective man might ask how the whole basis of modern western civilization could have been so quickly overturned. Whatever people are asking, the Church must be prepared and equipped to engage with their questions. John Stott coined the phrase 'double listening' in the early 1980s, saying Christians must listen to the Word (the Bible) and listen to the world. Then we will be able to relate one to the other.

Preaching and teaching must help Christians to do that. Relating the Word to the world is a learned skill. Building for the gospel in any church must include the task of building in people's lives to equip them, as Christians, in the here and now to make this vital link: as Christian parents, as Christian colleagues, as Christian friends.

A church for today (with round pegs in round holes)

After the project was completed, Miles spent sabbatical leave studying the effects of commuting on the lives of church members. This phenomenon is a feature of church life and of family life right round the home counties. The sheer numbers who pile off the trains every evening, and often don't get home until late, mean midweek church life has its limitations. Churches need to get behind people in the hard places of business, commerce and education, and pray for them.[3] Tired commuters have little enough time with their families and may find home groups or other evening meetings just too hard to get to. Other ways need to be found of helping them to 'dialogue' with the Bible for themselves, to interrogate it, to prove it as a trustworthy and sufficient guide, both for the big questions and for everyday living.

Even before the undercroft was built, it was agreed in principle that the next step would be to recruit an additional member of the church staff. Not to do 'more of the same', but to get alongside the many leaders (in the children's work, youth work, home groups, weekly meetings...) to equip and resource them, and provide whatever on-the-job training and support they needed; and to keep a constant eye open for those with overload. He could also nurture a future generation of leaders. The job title was eventually agreed as Director of Pastoring and Training. It was to be an enabling job, a bit like that of a team coach. Someone nicknamed it 'church bodybuilder'. In the summer of 1997 Philip de Grey-Warter joined the staff in this role. Buildings are needed for effective ministry but having the right people in the right jobs, enabling that ministry, is just as vital.

With Philip on board, two major new initiatives have been possible. *First*, he and the other clergy are able to look out for rising leaders in whom time and training should be invested. Phil and his wife, Naomi, run a training course for groups of six or eight at a time, culminating in a residential weekend. Over a programme like this, the members get to know one another, and there is a team spirit of learning together. 'The aim,' says Philip, 'is to enthuse and envision members for biblical ministry and spiritual leadership, and begin to equip them for it.' As leaders, these people will themselves be building for the gospel in the lives of others. There is no pressure on anyone to take up a leadership role straight away, nor any pressure on Phil to put someone in a gap which needs to be plugged. It is vital to have these people in the right roles, working with children, teenagers, home groups or in another capacity. Gaps and spare bodies do not necessarily go together.

Secondly there is 'Toolbox'. Here, on an occasional basis, two or three evening services in a row are replaced by seminars on a range of subjects. These seminars look at the practical aspects of what it means to be a Christian in the world of business, commerce, and education; in the family; in the community. 'This has been an experiment in finding an appropriate, new way to *be* church,' says Philip. 'We believe the good news of Jesus Christ is life-transforming, and we want to help people make the connection between the gospel and day-to-day life. For me, there's no greater thrill than seeing someone grasp the difference Jesus makes, and live it out distinctively and attractively.'

It would be misleading to say there is no evening worship on those Sundays, for the whole evening is an act of worship, as church members seek to work out the Lordship of Christ in their lives.

In 1998, three local businessmen who had met regularly for several years to pray for Sevenoaks, approached Miles. They wanted to see a clear Christian witness for those who worked in the town. This has grown into an established monthly meeting held in St Nicholas. After lunch together in the undercroft, there is a chance to study the Bible together. The church's proximity to the town centre has made it an ideal venue. Some who come have no church links at all; others are from one or another church in the area.

in a world of fragmented thinking, to be reminded of things 'holding together' is profound

'Toolbox' and the lunchtime meeting for those working locally are just starters as St Nick's thinks through imaginative ways to make the best use of new premises. The overall aim is to nurture the life of Christ in people, the life of the One through whom everything was created, and in whom all things hold together.[4] In a world of fragmented and often disconnected thinking – disconnected from the present and disconnected from the past – to be reminded of things 'holding together' in Christ is profound.

The staff need to nurture those who have been Christians a matter of weeks, and others who have been Christians for decades. Contact leaders work at their teaching, and at its contemporary application, to engage the minds and hearts of a new generation of Contact members. For everyone, our grasp of the gospel and of its bearing on life and society always needs to be stretched. Building for the gospel will always bring fresh opportunities to every new generation in every culture. It will not be completed until the Lord Jesus returns.

Layabouts and slaves?

For a long time, St Nick's had been welcoming a new graduate onto the staff team for a year at a time, as an extra pair of hands. The role of the lay assistant had come to include moving chairs, cleaning the loos, speaking at school assemblies and Christian Unions, helping lead Centrepoint and Contact, and being a general factotum right across the life of the church family. It was unglamorous, and depended very much on a serving heart. Given the pressures on those who led the children's and young people's work, the lay assistant was also able to relieve them of tasks like shopping and cooking for the Contact suppers or arranging the Centrepoint weekend away. Versatility was the name of the game.

B for the G had resulted in new initiatives in the undercroft, and in more people coming to midweek events, as well as to Sunday services. There were more ministry opportunities, and consequently more help was needed. So the PCC decided to have two lay assistants from then on, ideally one of each sex. They are given board, and a minimal income. It is, in effect, a training year, and their weekly schedule incorporates some structured study. This aspect of personal spiritual development is an integrated part of the whole. Some lay assistants go on into ordained ministry; others to service overseas. Whether they are preparing for that, or to serve Christ in a secular profession, a year like this often proves to be one of significance.

There is now a growing network of evangelical churches offering an internship. St Ebbe's in Oxford used to nickname its lay assistants 'layabouts', but, perhaps for fear of a massive surge in applicants(!) started to call them 'apprentices' to reflect more truly the learning aspect of the job, which is so central. St Helen's, Bishopsgate, in London, for a long time called theirs 'slaves'! Terminology apart, this is a unique chance to see Christian ministry from the inside, and to learn on the job, while also serving.[5]

Chapter 10

Welcome to St Nick's! – A church without a congregation

The word 'congregation' has inevitably slipped into the pages of this book from time to time. It is a useful word. In every church in the land, people congregate on a Sunday morning; they gather together. In that sense, St Nicholas has a 'congregation'. But it is a word rarely used in church life. The term accurately describes the state of a group of people, having come together, but it does not indicate any purpose for their doing so, nor any relationship between them. It is a neutral, even 'static' word. St Nicholas does not '*have* a congregation'. It '*is* a church family'.

Unity in diversity

In the rows of chairs on any Sunday, there is a mix of elderly, middle-aged and young; married and single; high earners and more modest earners and unemployed. Most are committed Christians; some are still looking tentatively into the Christian faith, and joining in the Sunday services as they do so. All are included in the 'church family'.

St Nicholas is an Anglican church with an Anglican heritage as long as any in the land, having been on the same site since before the Reformation. Its service book *St Nicholas Praise* follows a simplified Anglican liturgy. But an increasing number of its members were not brought up in the Anglican church. They may have grown up in Christian families from a different tradition or they may have come to faith as students, or as adults, from no Christian background at all. Every year, as new members are confirmed, there are those among them who were not baptised as infants. So they are baptised as adult believers on the preceding Sunday. It is not at all unusual for this to happen, and these are moving occasions.

John Buckeridge, Editor of *Youthwork* magazine, summed up the essence of Christian ministry in the words, 'The main thing is to keep the main thing the main thing. That's the main thing.' Simple, and right to the point. St Nick's aims to do that. And what is the main thing? In a nutshell, it is to worship God the Father, and the risen Lord Jesus Christ through the power of the Holy Spirit; to help one another to grow in the faith; and to make God's truth better known to those outside the church. These are all intertwined as triple biblical priorities. They are 'the main thing'.

Some people prefer older hymns; some prefer modern songs. This is a matter of style, not of substance; it reflects a mixture of Christian background and tradition, musical taste and aspects of people's personalities. When *St Nicholas Praise* was first brought out, it was never intended to last long. Its photocopied pages held together with a slide binder were the ideal means of presentation. 'From the outset,' said Miles, 'we agreed that we would produce something that is bin-able.' From year to year, hymn writers like Christopher Idle, Timothy Dudley-Smith and Graham Kendrick are producing new hymns and songs which grow out of our contemporary culture in the way that Wesley's did out of his. It is usually obvious from the start whether or not a new hymn will stand the test of time. Where lasting truth is expressed in a modern melody with a singable rhythm, it would be regrettable not to introduce it for Sunday worship. So *St Nicholas Praise* complements the hymn book and is revised from time to time. The main Sunday services incorporate this range of older hymns, newer hymns and modern songs; some are accompanied by the organist, and others by a keyboard player and a small band of musicians.

While there is still a place for Holy Communion following the Book of Common Prayer, this is held as a separate service on a Sunday morning at eight o'clock.

Mothers, nannies, young children

The church family includes many mothers with young children. As well as having a crèche on Sunday mornings, so mothers can be part of the church service, there are other events in the week especially for them. A Bible study group for mothers meets fortnightly in school term time. Then once a month, women of all ages gather to discuss aspects of contemporary living, and how to give biblical answers to questions raised by their friends.

Hoping for a ride on the blue whale in the crèche

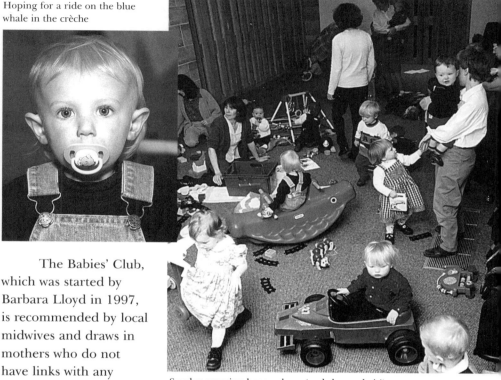

Sunday morning happy chaos (and she made it!)

The Babies' Club, which was started by Barbara Lloyd in 1997, is recommended by local midwives and draws in mothers who do not have links with any church. Many career women have carried on working as late as they can, and find the new lifestyle of motherhood very isolating, and one for which they have been given no preparation. The incidence of post-natal depression in commuter areas is often high, with the sudden switch from professional life to full-time motherhood as a contributory factor. The Babies' Club acts as a support group for new mothers in particular, and for some nannies. For those who want to explore the Christian faith, or to think about baptism, there is the chance to do so, but with no pressure. When this group meets, the entrance to the room they use in the undercroft is an obstacle course of pushchairs and prams. Babies 'graduate' from this to Mum & Co on their first birthday.

Mum & Co is so named, as, like the Babies' Club, it includes nannies

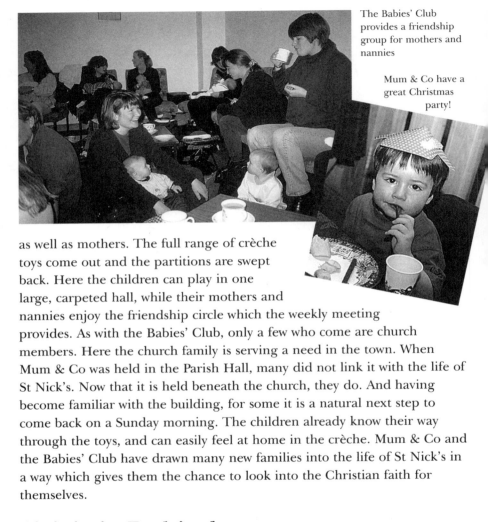

The Babies' Club provides a friendship group for mothers and nannies

Mum & Co have a great Christmas party!

as well as mothers. The full range of crèche toys come out and the partitions are swept back. Here the children can play in one large, carpeted hall, while their mothers and nannies enjoy the friendship circle which the weekly meeting provides. As with the Babies' Club, only a few who come are church members. Here the church family is serving a need in the town. When Mum & Co was held in the Parish Hall, many did not link it with the life of St Nick's. Now that it is held beneath the church, they do. And having become familiar with the building, for some it is a natural next step to come back on a Sunday morning. The children already know their way through the toys, and can easily feel at home in the crèche. Mum & Co and the Babies' Club have drawn many new families into the life of St Nick's in a way which gives them the chance to look into the Christian faith for themselves.

Christianity Explained

National initiatives for introducing people to the Christian faith have received mixed publicity. St Nick's runs 'Christianity Explained', a six-week discussion course. There are no questions barred. It is a chance to explore Christian teaching together, in an unhurried manner and an unpressured environment. The courses run three or four times a year. Some who come have already joined the church family in Sunday services; others have not.

Mark Standen, now Rector of St Margaret's, Angmering, in West Sussex, launched the course in 1998. Summing up its first year, he said, 'People have wanted to know the answers to some very searching questions like 'How can a God of love and power allow so much misery and chaos in the world?'; 'What happens when I die?'; 'Is Jesus really the only way to God?' In the group we try to address these, and to explain simply and clearly what it means to be a Christian.'

Whereas members are encouraged to come to all the meetings, there is no pressure to do so; in a town where commuters give so much of their energy to the working day, a commitment like that can be impossible.

Contact

This group of senior school pupils – and students while back at home - is an integral part of the St Nick's family. Some have grown up in the church; others have come into the group with no Christian background at all. The lay assistants, being fairly close in age while having some critical years of experience behind them, can get alongside Contact as older friends. Contact members are part of church life, and on a Sunday morning several help with the children's work. On a Sunday evening they form a solid block at the back of the south aisle and move *en masse* downstairs to the undercroft at the end of the service. Often a Contact member will read the lesson, or a group from Contact lead the evening prayers; a few members play in the music group. It is, by nature, a transient company, and each year a third moves off, mainly to college and university, and a new bunch from Centrepoint braves the south aisle.

Contact leaders stay in touch with their former members as much as they are able to. For students, this link by letter or email with a home church can mean a great deal. When terms finish, and students arrive back home, they are publicly welcomed by whoever is leading the service. As families include different generations, so Contact is the younger generation of the church family. They would be greatly missed if they weren't there. Every year, some former members come back to help lead the annual Contact houseparty. In this way, students can put into practice the leadership skills they have been learning through the student Christian

Family service: the grown-ups need to consult but the children know the answer!

Union or Navigator groups, in a spirit of service.

The 'gap year', which increased in popularity so rapidly in the early 1990s, offers everything under the sun. This can be a year between school and college, or between graduation and getting a job, or sometimes a year midway through a course. About two-thirds of Contact members take gap years, many using this time to travel, not just as sightseers, but in far more interesting ways. Some have worked alongside missionaries in Asia, Africa or Europe; others have brought practical skills to building work on different continents. Of those who have used part of the time in Christian service, not everyone has gone overseas: some have worked in needier parts of the UK with the London City Mission or with Careforce. But whatever Contact members have done, most have begun their gap year in the same way: by earning money to fund themselves.

Learning together

In his letters to young churches in the New Testament, the apostle Paul laid a lot of emphasis on growing in the faith. The life of St Nick's aims to help people do that. As well as the Bible teaching on Sundays, there are home groups. In the relaxed setting of church members' homes, and under the guidance of the church staff, they work through a study course, based on a book of the Bible, or they look at a contemporary issue. Whatever the approach, the aim is to work at applying biblical principles to every area of life. As a smaller group within the larger church family, they also provide support and fellowship with an opportunity to talk and pray together, and the chance for occasional social events.

The mothers' Bible study group is another example of an opportunity to learn from the Bible, and from one another. Then there are Saturday men's breakfasts and women's breakfasts, especially valuable for those who cannot get to midweek meetings because of work demands. These sometimes include a talk from an outside speaker, otherwise there is discussion around the table. Again, the issues raised are brought to the cutting edge of Scripture, and together people work out how to apply its eternal principles to the here and now. Saturdays are always precious times for families, so breakfast finishes punctually at ten o'clock.

The 'Retired men's think it through' meets once a month in the Rectory. Here, retired men can look at the claims of Christ, and at what it means to believe in him. Some recall Bible verses they memorized in school, but they may never have been taught how the parts of the Bible fit together. The retired men's lunches held throughout the winter set this group in a wider context of friendship, with an annual outing.

Houseparties

People get to know one another well when they have time to talk over meals, play sport and generally relax together. Every year St Nick's has a houseparty, either for a weekend or for a whole week, to help this happen. The timetable is partly structured, and mainly not. If people want an early-morning swim, they can have it. However, for most people, their first public appearance is at breakfast. The daily programme begins with Bible teaching, either from a member of the staff team or from a visiting speaker. God's Word is at the centre of St Nick's life, and the houseparty gives a chance to stand back from the hurly-burly of the every day and look at a book or a theme.

The children have their own programme, so parents can relax and not feel they have to keep an eye on them or an ear open for them.

Every houseparty includes some who have been 'regulars' since they

The annual barbecue: smells promising!

began in the 1970s, and others for whom it is their first. The thought of going away for a week, or even for a weekend, with a lot of people one does not know, can be quite daunting for newcomers, but it often proves a time to make or cement friendships. Sam Berry, Professor of Genetics at London University, and his wife, Caroline, a medical consultant, have been on St Nicholas houseparty weekends since they first started. Reflecting on their value, Sam said: 'Most of the early churches in the New Testament were probably small enough for members to get to know each other and do things together. Houseparties, like home groups, help people form the kind of bonds which characterize an extended family. They're a great way of drawing in newcomers, they're fun, and they're a key part of the life of a large church like St Nick's.'

The bookshop and coffee shop

The undercroft bookshop and coffee shop is open during the week, and run largely by volunteers, under part-time management. With a car park right behind the church, it is easy to get to, and any book which is not in stock can be ordered quickly. There is a good selection of children's books, and of cards, and there are staff on hand who can make suggestions on, for example, what to buy for a baptism or confirmation present, or for a child's birthday.

B for the G in our postmodern world

Despite all the media hype over the millennium, a surprising proportion of people do not realize that it marks a uniquely Christian event in history. That may be ironic, and a tragic comment on our education system as well as on the Church, but it is a fact we must work from, and not just lament.

Good books have been written by shrewd observers on how our culture is changing, and on what post-modernity means for thought patterns, attitudes to truth and to authority, methods of teaching, and emotional expectations. Some secular writers have been very perceptive and we do well to learn from them as we think through the implications for spiritual nurture and for evangelism. It is beyond the remit of this book to explore those avenues, but any church seriously wanting to present the ever-contemporary gospel in a contemporary way, will have to give thought to its buildings.

Amusing ourselves to Death by Neil Postman (Heinemann, 1986) may not be new, but is still well worth reading. To get a feel for the thought patterns of Generation X, read *Generation X* or anything else by Douglas Coupland (Simon and Schuster). For a Christian analysis of how to relate to Generation X, read *A Generation Alone* by William Mahedy and Janet Bernardi (IVP, 1994). Phil Hill's *The Church of the Third Millennium* (OM Publishing,1999) looks at how post-modernity impacts on the church.

Roy Clements' *Expository Preaching in a Postmodern World* (Cambridge Papers, 1998) is trenchant (email: cpapers@campublic.co.uk).

The Christian faith is a reasoned faith, and Christian books deepen our grasp of its truth, and its application in daily life. The bookshop carries titles for people looking tentatively at what the Christian faith is all about and books for committed Christians on practical issues like bringing up children, getting priorities right, coping with stress. Then there are Bibles, and Bible commentaries.

The coffee shop draws in tourists to the town, too. People come to buy books, to have something to eat, or just to have a chat.

It has also proved a successful venue for *ad hoc* events like an authors' evening, where new books are launched, or for coffee and dessert as people arrive to hear a speaker. And some couples from the church have used its facilities for their wedding reception.

St Nicholas around the world

The missionaries sent out by St Nicholas are not its only ambassadors around the world. There are often families from the church in Africa, Asia or Europe for spells of two or three years, and some who deliberately take their professions to an Islamic land, often for a much longer time. The missionaries send newsletters home every two or three months and copies are distributed to all who want to receive them. Keeping communication links is all-important in church family life.

Adding together the church's missionaries, people working overseas, and Contact members on short-term mission projects, brings the number of countries across which the St Nick's family extends to twelve or fifteen at any one time.

Caring for one another

Wendy Billington, the church pastoral assistant, leads the Care Committee. This is a small group of people who work to facilitate care for those in need. For example, if someone living alone is ill, the most practical thing to do might be to take round a hot meal. Or if a mother is in hospital, some frozen meals for the family could be appreciated. Or if elderly people need a lift to church or help with their shopping, these practicalities are addressed.

The Care Committee encourages mutual care, and praying for one another. Where a person has gone through a period of unemployment, and might be a help to someone else facing this, the Committee will put them in touch. As well as this, the unemployed all meet together from time to time to pray, to share their news, and to offer each other support. If there are widows or widowers who have come through their own deep grief, and could offer an understanding ear to others in earlier stages of bereavement, then again, this is facilitated.

The weekly Tuesday Fellowship for senior women in St Nick's, and the meetings for retired men described earlier, provide another valuable network of support and friendship. It is not unusual for those who have recently lost their husband or wife to start coming to these groups, even if they have no other church links. For several it has been the means of their being drawn into the church family, and coming to a living faith in Christ.

Getting past the crowds on a Sunday

Sunday services are often full, and new people could get lost in the crowd. The churchwardens, assisted by a welcome team, try to make sure this doesn't happen. A church family should welcome visitors into their church building, as a family welcomes visitors into its home.

For those who want to talk privately about something on their minds, or to have someone pray with them, there are people ready to do that. This is open to anyone who might want to talk or pray about anything; it does not need to be a major life-crisis. Members of the prayer team make themselves available after services at the front of the south aisle, where people can go and sit with them out of the public eye, and talk confidentially.

A sense of dynamic

St Nicholas members, then, do more than 'congregate'. There is a sense of dynamic about church life, and the apostle Paul's constant references to 'one another' are to be taken seriously in this connection. His letters to the New Testament churches reflect a perceptive grasp of human weakness, and of spiritual aspiration.

The famous Victorian preacher, Charles Haddon Spurgeon, coined the phrase 'bibline blood'. He wanted his own church family, at the Metropolitan Tabernacle in London's Elephant and Castle, to get the Bible into their bloodstreams – so to speak; into the way they thought and acted and related to each other. That is the spirit of Paul's writing. Biblical values which become the 'pulse' of day-to-day living.

Like any other church, St Nick's has a long way to go and will always have to keep on working at these things. ❧

Chapter 11

For any churches that are wavering

Churches in many towns and cities have been struggling with big decisions about their buildings over the past 20 years, and others will do so over the next 20 years. Church leaders have seen – and understood - reticence, even fear, among their congregations when ideas for extending or re-ordering have first been aired. For everyone, finance is a major consideration. Children and teenagers make ever-heavier demands on the family budget to supply them with whatever their friends have, and Christian parents naturally find themselves pulled in several directions. For single people the pressures are different, but no less real.

It is part of our culture to live at the extreme edge of our means, or slightly beyond that. What does it mean to 'afford' to give? How can we have faith that others will also give sacrificially, to make our own giving worthwhile? Do we really *need* better buildings anyway, or can we 'make do'? Some questions are genuine; others spring from a desire to protect our own, or our families', financial interests from what may be perceived as a threat.

Adventures of faith demand faith. And there can be times when that faith is not easy to maintain. The Christian life is often described as 'a fight of faith'. From the inside it can seem more like 'a fight *for* faith'. Miles sent a note to the St Nicholas PCC three years after they had first agreed to allow research into the possibilities of digging underneath the building to go ahead. Things were moving so slowly, and it would be a further four years before the work started. He wrote:

> The Awayday we had in October 1988 seems a long time ago, when we decided to research the feasibility of an undercroft. Since then there's been much prayer, debate and research - as well as butterflies in the stomach. Now we're inviting ourselves and the church family to rise to the challenge. I guess we all feel we're treading water at 60 feet! Last week someone said he felt this challenge is one of the greatest this church has faced in its history. I think that may be right.

That throws me back to Nehemiah. I've re-read the first four chapters and how the Lord wonderfully worked. Concern turned into prayer, and prayer led to taking a risk. Together there was careful research and confidence in God, in the face first of ridicule, then of opposition. Nehemiah has become a good friend. I've learned much in these past three years. As God was with Nehemiah and the people then, we can trust him to be with us today. 'Everything that was written in the past was written to teach us... (Romans 15:4) This is our God, and we want to make him better known across our parish and our town.

'Everything that was written in the past is written to teach us.' For evangelical churches, where leaders and members alike hold a high view of Scripture, its rock solid truth is something to lean on. Miles and the churchwardens would be the first to say that they could not have succeeded without its sure promises. But that begs another question. Would they have started without them? No. It was an act of obedience to move ahead – a *response* to all that the Bible teaches of our inheritance in Christ, and our joyful privilege of sharing the gospel with others.

Carrying a church family over such a process is demanding. Staff and wardens need prayer as they shoulder the responsibility, and continue to pastor those in their charge: the ones who are supportive; the ones who are indifferent; the ones who are negative.

Keeping in touch with other churches at similar stages on this long road can be very helpful. St Nicholas has had a close link with All Saints, Crowborough in East Sussex, since Andrew Cornes and his PCC started to explore a major building project. For them, as for St Nick's, there have been difficulties. Some members have left because they genuinely could not feel comfortable with the expenditure, and there has been the same kind of local opposition as there was in Sevenoaks. When news arrived that sufficient funding had come in for work to begin, the church family in Sevenoaks rejoiced with the church family 20 miles away. That is 'fellowship in the gospel'.

Looking around the country, the work is now 'Done' in some places; for others it still seems 'Impossible'. If your church is looking at a major project, you might like to visit a place which has reached 'Done' and talk honestly about the 'Impossible' and 'Difficult' staging posts.

Cambridge – Done!

Holy Trinity in Cambridge re-ordered its building in the early 1980s, under the leadership of Michael Rees. This church, situated opposite Woolworth's in the centre of the world-famous university town, has special significance in evangelical history. In common with St Nicholas, if it was to maximize its usefulness, it needed to change.

Though undoubtedly pleasing, it is not striking architecturally, and with King's College Chapel and Great St Mary's just a hundred yards away, it could easily be overlooked by tourists. Charles Simeon, converted as a new student at King's College, became its vicar in 1782 when he was just 23 years old, and stayed there for 54 years. The congregation hated his preaching, which was simple and unequivocal Bible teaching, and the churchwardens at one stage locked him out of the building! His umbrella (one of the first in England) and teapot (used for 18th century evangelistic tea parties) are still to be seen there. Simeon played a key role in establishing several major missionary societies, and his own emphasis on training ordinands was to prove seminal. Henry Martyn, the highly gifted Cambridge mathematician who was senior wrangler of his year, became Simeon's curate. Martyn went on to translate Scripture into Urdu, Persian and Arabic, dying at the age of 31 in 1812.

The church draws crowds of students on a Sunday, and the university pastorate is based on it. Simeon had set the standard, and there has been a long tradition of evangelical preaching there since, from which 'town and gown' have both benefited.

Any major re-ordering costs a significant sum, and generous giving is needed from salaried people to meet that. Michael Rees, now Missioner in the Chester Diocese, recalls how students led the way. 'Students started to put paper money in the plates, and this encouraged the regular church members to think again about their giving levels.'

Around the corner from Holy Trinity is the church of St Andrew the Great. It had been lying empty when the 'The Round' Church (more properly – though somewhat rarely – known as the Church of the Holy Sepulchre) had outgrown its building, and had started to meet in the Cambridge Union debating chamber. The Round was, as Mark Ashton, its vicar, described it, 'a quaint circular Norman building with a medieval oblong tacked on to it'. With large crowds of students coming to Sunday services, doubling and halving the congregation as terms started then finished, various solutions to the 'problem' had been explored. They tried a television relay around the Norman pillars with an overflow relay in the church hall, using another church building, and finally the move to the Union.

The debating chamber proved a much better venue than the Round, but there was no security of tenure, and the Union Society had made it clear all along that procuring a 'big name' speaker at short notice could mean a short-notice cancellation for services on any Sunday. In the event, this never happened, but it underlined the need for decisive action.

The availability of St Andrew the Great seemed very attractive. It could provide seating for over 700 people, with ten ancillary rooms for other activities. As with Holy Trinity, The Round had close links with the Cambridge Inter-Collegiate Christian Union (CICCU), and greater space would enable more creative ways of serving the students as well as the growing number of young families who were coming regularly. But it would cost £1,800,000 to do the work.

While the church met in the Union, its leaders had taken the opportunity of thinking through their theology of Sunday worship. Christians come together to worship the living God, and a right sense of awe and transcendence should characterize that. But the 'one another' focus is also central. 'The key New Testament word used for Christians meeting together,' says Mark Ashton, 'is edification, not worship. It is interesting that it is a "building" word, but with an entirely "people" sense.'[1] Having this in mind meant they were able to relate that to the design of St Andrew the Great. This building project in Cambridge began while St Nick's was 'in exile' but managed to leapfrog, moving into its new building first!

Glasgow – Moving from Impossible to Difficult

On the eastern outskirts of Glasgow, Chryston Parish Church has some 900 on its communion role, and a spacious church building with a gallery. It owns two church halls, a Boys' Brigade hall, and a church officer's house, as well as a manse. In the early 1980s, repair work was needed to make safe the church building, then over a hundred years old; this prompted some radical discussion about the future of the premises. In September 1982, under the leadership of Martin Allen, the Congregational Board[2] put forward the idea of demolishing one of the two church halls, and making the church building itself more flexible, with a sanctuary upstairs and a suite of halls underneath. The cost was estimated at £220,000. However the congregation voted against this recommendation by 186 votes to 141.

Two months later, in November 1982, there was another church meeting. Eighty per cent of those present voted in favour of a less-ambitious plan, namely repairing the church building and upgrading the hall, working within a budget of £175,000. The issue had by this stage already raised a lot of tension and division.

In the Church of Scotland, all major building projects have to be approved by the local Presbytery and the Glasgow Presbytery[3] Buildings Committee had examined and approved the earlier plans put forward by the Congregational Board. On the strength of that, it was assumed that the whole Presbytery would prefer and recommend this more ambitious and radical course of action. However church members who were not happy made representation at the critical meeting, and, by a narrow majority, the Presbytery decided not to support it.

Lines seemed to have been drawn between 'in-comers' and 'locals' and between those perceived as 'the progressives' and those seen as 'the traditionalists'. However, after the Presbytery decision was made, people rallied in a wonderful way, and worked together to meet the target figure for the second option. Unity in the gospel was of far greater importance than building plans and, with an act of will, the life and witness of the church continued. However, for some, it took a long time for healing to take place. The Building Fund was eventually to exceed what was needed, and almost all of this was by direct giving. It was a marvellous testimony to the way the church family pulled together, and this renovation work was completed in late 1983.

By 1996 a second morning service had started – in their Moodiesburn church hall, one and a half miles away, and this soon drew 120 people. Chryston Parish Church now had 250 coming in the morning, and around 150 in the evening. Problems of growth were starting to surface, and could not be ignored. God was drawing in people with little Christian background, who wanted to look at the claims of Christ for themselves. Already the buildings were unsuitable for the changing needs. It seemed a good time for the matter to be raised again.

In 1997 the Congregational Board recommended a three-phase plan, and this received good support from the church membership.

Phase 1 to demolish the second church hall
Phase 2 to extend the church officer's house, adjacent to the church, and convert it into a suite of meeting rooms
Phase 3 to remove the pews from downstairs in the church to make it more flexible for midweek use, and to upgrade the fabric of the Moodiesburn hall

The whole scheme would cost £160,000 of which £60,000 would be re-couped from the sale of the second church hall to a developer. However it was agreed that first a stewardship campaign be mounted to improve the general funding of the church.

That campaign, now completed, has seen an increase of over 30 per cent in general giving, and detailed plans are being drawn up for the first two phases as this book is published. Some differences are being voiced, but the prevailing view is that the buildings must be got right. 'The Church operates on a different timescale from the world,' says Martin Allen. 'It was not the appropriate moment in God's timetable 17 years ago for major changes in our buildings. Patience wasn't easy, but now a visionary scheme, achievable plans, and the will of the church members have harmonized. And we can look forward to buildings which meet the needs presented by a new century.'

Getting the right people

Tony Wilmot's enthusiasm gave a major thrust to the St Nicholas undercroft from the beginning. He brought a mix of spiritual aspiration, shrewd judgment and professional experience – a wonderful provision. Brigadier Ian Dobbie's availability in 1992 was surely also providential. His own spiritual values, his determination, his willingness, and his unusual background in managing people and in managing projects contributed

The mountain-climbing analogy

Building projects can be likened to climbing a steep mountain, as Paul Batchelor explained to members of the Round Church in Cambridge.

- In both, we have a clear objective in view and an unshakable guide.

- We know the route to take, and we have the best possible back-up team.

- There are obstacles to navigate from the earliest stages, and at times the going can be very tough. We know we can trust our guide, but we still at times experience doubt and fear. Sometimes we feel like giving up and turning back.

- As we look back we snatch a glimpse of the view. We can see some progress has been made. The end seems more worthwhile, and the seemingly 'impossible' becomes the 'very difficult'.

- We must keep the summit in our mind's eye, even when clouds descend. People have made financial sacrifices, and are honouring their promises. We remember this, and we think of the spiritual benefits that reaching the summit – gaining the new facilities – will offer. It spurs us on.

- The summit seems closer, then recedes. We suddenly meet a new difficulty, another long haul, which we had not anticipated.

- We have to accept that not everyone in the group will make equal progress. Doubt can keep creeping back, and for some this will be a genuine impediment. How vital for the leaders to trust the guide implicitly, and to take others with them in that.

- Every so often, pause for rest and refreshment, take a look at the view and remind yourself of progress made. But don't loiter too long.

- For success in climbing a difficult mountain, we need to dig deep into resources of stamina and energy. To keep our eyes on the summit will take all our spiritual reserves.

- Once the summit is reached, we can see other mountains to climb, stretching out ahead, which were previously not in view.

hugely. They were God's people for those roles.

From the outset Miles and the churchwardens knew that several 'right people' would be needed for the building committee and the Finance Advisory Group, and several more for a range of ancillary roles. People with the right gifts, the right commitment to the task, and the same spiritual values. In any position, a wrong choice of person could hamper proceedings. All the world over, able people are often the busiest, and church leaders can feel reticent about approaching those who are already heavily committed. St Nicholas was no different. It faced the same question every church faces at this critical, early planning stage. Namely, who would do the work?

On the basis that people have to make their own decisions before God, the policy Miles adopted was to approach those with suitable gifts and qualities to consider openings. He then trusted their judgment as to what they could take on. He made it clear that he was not putting pressure on them, and that he realized they would have to consider the matter carefully.

In 1991 the *B for the G* treasurer asked to stand down. So a further 'right person' was needed. As Miles and the churchwardens began to think and pray about a successor, Paul Batchelor seemed an obvious choice. So Miles called on him. He and Janet were about to leave for India, to visit their daughter who was spending her gap year teaching English there. He promised to think and pray about it while they were away, and he concluded it was right to accept.

Just over a year later, Paul spoke to members of the Round Church one Saturday afternoon. They were, at that stage, still considering whether or not to go ahead with their move to St Andrew the Great. He was open with them about his own early misgivings. He was frank, too, about his hesitation when asked to become treasurer. In recalling this, Paul noted two things as important in his decision. *First*, he could see no viable alternative to digging underneath St Nicholas, with all the expense that would incur; *secondly*, he had begun to reflect on the sacrifices which his forebears had made to create the building which was now standing. Perhaps, he felt, it *was* the present generation's task to do something for those who would follow.

Paul had many calls on his time professionally, and Janet suffered as much as anyone from his demanding schedule. But as they were now convinced of the need for integrated facilities, they knew they had to do more than just give money. Paul had handled several major construction projects overseas, and he felt this was a God-given talent to be pressed into service.

'Our involvement has strengthened our faith, and our understanding of what faith means,' Paul told the Round congregation. 'Giving what is most precious – in my case time – is what sacrificial giving is about.' He had grown up in a Kent village where his father co-ordinated efforts to have the church rebuilt after it was destroyed by a German flying bomb. That team spirit had galvanized a small village community recovering from the war to raise £20,000. It had been an enormous undertaking. Now, Paul felt, it was his turn, and his privilege, to do something for future generations.

He closed by quoting from the apostle Paul's letter to the church in Ephesus, back in AD60. The thrust of the verses was to exhort the Ephesian Christians to remember that, as part of God's worldwide and eternal Church, they are *themselves* like a building, with Jesus Christ as the foundation stone. The passage concludes:

> In him the whole building is joined together and rises to become a holy temple to the Lord. And in him you too are being built together to become a dwelling in which God lives by his Spirit.

Paul Batchelor, then, took Paul the apostle's words, and related them directly to those in the room that Saturday afternoon. As with the church at Ephesus, so with The Round, and Holy Trinity, and St Nicholas, and Chryston. No church must ever get so preoccupied with its plant that it misses this central truth.

Fluctuating emotions

B for the G was a big adventure of faith. There were times when those under the most pressure wished they had never started on the undercroft. But when they turned back to Scripture, and to God's promises, things took on a truer perspective again. It was doubtless the same for Michael Baughen and his team in All Souls, Langham Place, and for Michael Rees in Holy Trinity, Cambridge. It will be the same for Chryston, and for Cleo's, and for Crowborough. Every church embarking on this particular 'fight of faith' will, to put it positively, find new ways to prove God's faithfulness.

From the launch of the project in June 1991 up to April 1993 when the final designs and tender documents were complete, there were constantly fluctuating emotions. Progress on one front would, it seemed, quickly be followed by a new obstacle somewhere else.

All sorts of things jostled together, demanding the building committee's attention. There were technical questions of design and engineering. There was the financial aspect of monitoring the income, and deciding when to launch another phase or facet of the appeal. Communication with the church family and with the media was vital all the way. Dealing with questions, objections, doubters, diocesan authorities, archaeologists and conservationists... It was no enviable task, but they had 'put their hands to the plough' and, with help, were enabled not to turn back.

'We were sustained throughout this period by prayer, and the certain knowledge that God's will would prevail in his own good time,' said a member of the building committee. 'There were many moments of uncertainty, and a few of great uncertainty veering near despair, but renewed hope followed.' As the building committee members faced particular difficulties, their families inevitably felt the pressure too. The wife of one member recalled, several years later, how she had been helped in a prayer meeting by Terry Boxall's comments on a verse from James 1: 'Consider it pure joy whenever you face trials of many kinds.' She said, 'I can still picture where I was sitting, and I remember hearing that, and finding it so helpful at a time when there seemed to be great difficulties. It was one of the passages I learned the truth of through *B for the G*.'

An adventure of faith

Hudson Taylor's words once again apply: 'God's work done in God's way will never lack supply.' Surely that does not apply just to finance. It also applies to people for the task, and spiritual, physical and emotional resources to keep going. As he prayed for new workers, he never imagined that the way ahead would be trouble-free. His team of recruits in China, without even any formal language training, was derided in the House of Commons as 'the pigtail mission'; and there was homesickness and lack of trust among those who found it difficult to accept his authority. Years later, just as he was to hand over office as General Director of the mission, his chosen successor died – with over 50 others – in the cruel Boxer uprising. Hudson Taylor was not naïve.

Where would Miles direct people for help, to give them the stickability needed for a project which might take several years, as the undercroft did? As these pages reflect, there were several passages on different occasions which brought spiritual help and resolve. But if he were to single out one book of the Bible which gave both transferable principles and practical advice, it would be Nehemiah. Perhaps this is not surprising, as different parts of the Bible serve different purposes, and Nehemiah has

' Nehemiah has become one of my heroes'

been described as the book for those who want to achieve great things. The staff team preached through it twice over the course of B for the G, once on Sunday mornings, and once on Sunday evenings. There was help there for those at the sharp end, and help, too, for the whole church family. The emphasis throughout is of working *together*, and that was a crucial factor in creating the undercroft. In one chapter alone, as Nehemiah describes the position of people rebuilding the wall, the words 'next to him' appear over 20 times. Each person's role was vital. No-one's contribution went unnoticed.

'Nehemiah,' said Miles, 'has become one of my heroes. He led God's people through a remarkable rebuilding programme in the sixth century BC, rebuilding a people as well as a city. This book – hidden away in the middle of the Old Testament – provided us with some key principles in Building for the Gospel. These seem to come in pairs – balancing one another.

- *Prayer and commitment*. While the project grew out of his prayers, Nehemiah was willing to be the answer to his prayers (chapter 1). Hudson

Taylor's son said of his father, 'He prayed about things as if everything depended upon the praying. But he worked also, as if everything depended on the working.'

- *Vision and planning*. He was spurred on by a vision for this rebuilding. At the same time he did his homework: doing his research, surveying the situation and making plans (chapter 2).

- *Leader and members*. Nehemiah was a team-player and he involved all God's people in the project. This comes out clearly in chapter 3, where the phrase 'next to him' appears at least 20 times.

- *Sword and spade*. There were enemies around who were out to stop the rebuilding. Some opposition came from outside, some from inside, as God's people began to grumble under the pressure of the project. But nothing would be allowed to stop the work going forward. So they took a sword in one hand and a spade in the other (chapters 4-6).

- *Walls and people*. Rebuilding the walls was the prelude to rebuilding the people – in a new commitment to their Lord (chapters 7-13).

'Time and time again, turning to Nehemiah steadied our nerve and kept us to our vision. As this book reflects, we had, from the outset, committed ourselves not only to build a building, but also to 'build a people'. To build a church family who live under the authority of God's Word in God's world. It is still our prayer to keep on growing in faith as well as increasing in numbers, and to keep on training people for service – both in this country and overseas.

'We want to see more people here in Sevenoaks finding a personal faith in Christ, and growing in their knowledge and love of him. We want to see more taking Scripture as their guide at school or college and in business, commerce, education or health; more going into pastoral ministry; more working to build God's church worldwide. We thank God for all the ways we are already seeing this happen; we pray he will enable us to carry on 'Building for the Gospel' into a new century.'

Now to him who is able to do immeasurably more than all we ask or imagine, according to his power that is at work within us, to him be glory in the church and in Christ Jesus throughout all generations, for ever and ever! Amen.

Afterword

John Stott, widely known writer and speaker, and Rector Emeritus of All Souls, Langham Place, London, asks what God intends a church to be and to do.

I was delighted to see the fantastic St Nicholas undercroft. Congratulations on its conclusion. I know already it is proving more than you expected it to be. It has been a great lesson to many other churches throughout the country.

With your restructuring and re-ordering of St Nicholas, I am sure you have been asking in recent days what the Church is intended to be, what God means it for. It is a very important question, and I want to try to answer it from the Bible.

What is this new community of Jesus Christ intended to look like? What should its principal distinguishing marks be? I would love us to sit down alongside one another and see what answers we could get to those questions. It seems to me that one of the best ways to answer them is to take a fresh look at the first Christian community that came into being, in Jerusalem at Pentecost. But let's be realistic. There is a tendency to romanticise the early Church. To look back at it through coloured spectacles, and speak of it with bated breath, as if it had no blemishes. And we miss the hypocrisies, and the heresies, and the rivalries, and the immoralities which troubled the Church in those days as they trouble the Church today.

But one thing is absolutely clear. In spite of the excesses and the extravagancies in the early Church, it was radically moved by the Holy Spirit. So what did that first Spirit-filled and renewed church look like? What evidence did it give of the presence and power of the Holy Spirit in its life? If we can answer that question about the first church in Jerusalem, we are well on our way to finding what the marks of a renewed church would be today.

In Acts 2:42-47 we read:

'[The Christians] devoted themselves to the apostles' teaching and to the fellowship, to the breaking of bread and to prayer. Everyone was filled with awe, and many wonders and miraculous signs were done by the apostles. All the believers were together and had everything in common. Selling their possessions and goods, they gave to anyone as he had need. Every day they continued to meet together in the temple courts. They broke bread in their homes and ate together with glad and sincere hearts, praising God and enjoying the favour of all the people. And the Lord added to their number daily those who were being saved.'

It is an idyllic picture of that first Christian community. Luke, who was telling the story, draws out at least four major marks of a renewed, or Spirit-filled church.

First, the renewed church is a learning church, a studying church.

'They devoted themselves to the teaching of the apostles.' That is the very first thing he tells us about them. The Holy Spirit, we might say, opened a school in Jerusalem on the day of Pentecost. The apostles were the teachers, whom Jesus had chosen and trained, and there were three thousand pupils in the kindergarten. It was a very remarkable situation. We know that those new Spirit-filled converts were not enjoying some mystical experience which led them to neglect their intellect, or to despise theology, or to stop thinking. On the contrary, they devoted themselves to the teaching of the apostles. Anti-intellectualism and the fulness of the Spirit are mutually incompatible. I have no hesitation in saying that, as the Holy Spirit is the Spirit of truth. So whenever he is in control, truth matters. Those early Christians did not suppose that they could dispense with earthly teachers, having received the Holy Spirit. They knew that Jesus had appointed the apostles to be the teachers of the church, and they submitted to the apostles' authority, which we see from Acts 2:43 was authenticated by miracles. And the major purpose of miracles, right through biblical history, has been to authenticate fresh stages of revelation.

So what is the application of this for today? How do we devote ourselves to the apostles' teaching when there are no apostles today? There are bishops and other kinds of church leaders, and there are pioneer missionaries and church planters. Maybe we should call their work 'apostolic ministry' (using the adjective, but reserving the noun for the 12 apostles and Paul and James and one or two others). If there were apostles today, we should have to add their teaching to the New Testament, and all the Church would have to believe it and obey it. Of course, you know the answer. The teaching of the apostles has come down to us in its definitive form in the New Testament. And that is the apostolic succession. It is the continuity of this apostolic doctrine made possible by the New Testament.

The ministers of a Spirit-filled church expound scripture from the pulpit; its parents teach their children out of the Scriptures; its members read and reflect on Scripture every day to grow into maturity in Christ. The Spirit of God leads the people of God to the Word of God. So the Spirit-filled church is a *learning* church.

Secondly, it is a caring church.
Its people love one another, support one another, and care for one another. The word for 'fellowship' here is *koinonia*. It expresses two complementary truths:

- what we share *in* together. That is, of course, the grace of God. The apostle John begins his first letter 'Our fellowship is with the Father and with his Son' and Paul adds 'the fellowship of the Holy Spirit'. So authentic fellowship is trinitarian fellowship.

- what we share *out* together. So it is not only what we *receive* together, but what we *give* together. *Koinonia* is the word Paul used for a collection of money he was organising. The adjective from this word means generous.

> All the believers were together and they had everything in common. They sold their possessions and their goods, and they gave to everyone as he had need.

This is very disturbing. These are verses we trip over rather quickly in order to get on. Does it mean that every Spirit-filled believer should follow this example literally? Did Jesus call his disciples to sell everything and share their goods with others? Some have thought so, and some have done so. I do not doubt that Jesus still calls a small minority of his followers to voluntary poverty. That was his calling of the rich young ruler, and of Francis of Assisi in the middle ages, and of Mother Teresa and her sisters of Charity in our lifetime. But it is not the calling of everybody.

The prohibition of private property is a Marxist and not a Christian doctrine. It is worth noting that even in Jerusalem the selling and the giving were voluntary. We see in verse 46 that they broke bread in their homes. So they had not all sold their homes and their furniture. When we come to the story of Ananias and Sapphira in Acts 5, their sin was not in keeping back part of the proceeds from the property they had sold. Their sin was in pretending to give the whole. It was deceit, not greed. As if to underline this, the apostle Peter said to them, 'Before you sold it, was it not your own? After you sold it, was it not at your disposal?'

Every Christian has to make a conscientious decision before God as to what to do with their property and with their money. Perhaps that brings a sigh of relief! Nevertheless, we must not avoid the challenge of these verses.

Those early Christians truly loved one another. That is not surprising, as love is the first fruit of the Spirit. In particular, they cared for their poor sisters and brothers, and they shared with them their goods and their homes. This principle of generous and voluntary sharing is one of permanent validity. The Christian community should be the first community in the world in which poverty has been completely abolished. You may be aware of the statistics made public a few years ago in the Brandt Commission Report. The number of destitute people in the world lacking the necessities for survival is about one thousand million – a fifth of the world's population. And the number of those who die of starvation every day is ten thousand. How can we live with these statistics? The Holy Spirit gives his people a tender social conscience. So those who live in affluent situations, as we in the west do, must simplify our economic lifestyle to some degree, not because we think it will solve the macro-economic problems of the world, but out of solidarity with the poor.

The Spirit-filled church is a generous church. Generosity is a mark of God himself. Grace is another word for generosity. Our God is a generous God. So his people must be generous too.

Thirdly, it is a worshipping church.

As we reflect on the worship of the early church, notice how balanced it is. It was both formal and informal. It met both in the temple and in homes. The Christians did not immediately abandon the institutional Church. I have no doubt they were anxious to reform it according to the gospel, and already they knew that its sacrifices had been fulfilled in the sacrifice of Christ, but they continued to attend the prayer services of the temple, which certainly had a measure of liturgy and formality.

They also met in one another's homes in which they let their hair down and had a music group and so on. There is an important lesson for us here. Young people are understandably impatient with the inherited structure of the church. And some churches are too conservative and resistant to any change. They are stuck in the mud, and the mud is set like concrete. Their favourite quotation is from the liturgy: 'As it was in the beginning, is now, and ever shall be, world without end.' We need to listen to the young. Every church council and committee should have representative young people on it. We should listen to them respectfully, but that doesn't mean we should always agree with them. Sometimes we have to remind them that the Holy Spirit's way with the institution of the Church is more the way of patient reform than of impatient rejection.

The early church had formal and informal, and we must not polarise between the structured and the unstructured, or between the traditional and the spontaneous, or between the more formal, dignified services in church, and the informal, liberated meetings in one another's homes. Why must we always polarise? We need them both. I know St Nick's has its home groups as well as its dignified services in the church.

The early church's worship was both formal and informal. It was also both joyful and reverent. There is no doubt about their joy. The Greek word in verse 46 means an exuberant form of joy. God had sent his Son into the world. God had sent his Spirit into their hearts. How could they not be joyful! The fruit of the Spirit is love, joy and peace. When I have been to some services in other parts of the world, I think I have come to a funeral by mistake. Everybody is dressed in black. Nobody smiles. Nobody talks. Nobody laughs. The hymns are played at a snail's pace, and the whole atmosphere is lugubrious. If I could overcome my Anglo-Saxon reserve, I would want to shout out, 'Cheer up!'

Christianity is a joyful religion, and every service should be a celebration of the mighty acts of God in Christ. I am so thankful that Archbishop Geoffrey Fisher said, shortly before he died, 'The longer I live, the more convinced I am that Christianity is one long shout of joy.' That's good, isn't it! Not bad for an Archbishop. And he was right.

Although the worship of the early church was joyful, it was never irreverent. And if some church services today are funereal, others are flippant. Verse 43 tells us that everyone was filled with awe. The living and holy God had visited Jerusalem. He was in their midst, and they bowed down before him in that mixture of wonder and humility that we call worship. So don't let us imagine that worship excludes rejoicing, or that rejoicing excludes reverence. We need to recover the balance of the early church's worship in these ways.

Fourthly, a renewed church is an evangelizing church.

Luke says they devoted themselves to study, fellowship and worship. These three are all marks of the interior life of the church. They tell us nothing about its compassion and outreach into the community. This illustrates the danger of isolating a text from its context. Millions of sermons have been preached from Acts 2:42. It is a favourite verse with preachers who want to talk about the Church. I venture to say that every one of them has been unbalanced. That verse on its own does not give a balanced picture. It depicts only the interior life of the church. What about the world outside in its colossal material and spiritual needs? Surely the church is concerned about the lonely, the lost, the oppressed, and not preoccupied only with its worship, its study and its fellowship? It is not until we come down to Acts 2:47 that we read 'the Lord added to their number day by day those who were being saved.'

There are some important lessons we can learn there about evangelism:

(i) The Lord Jesus himself did it. It was Jesus who added to their number. Now he delegates to the clergy the task of welcoming people into the visible church by baptism. But he reserved for himself the prerogative of welcoming people into the invisible church when they exercise faith in him. Only he can do that. Only he can open the eyes of the blind, unstop the ears of the deaf, and give life to dead souls. And in this very self-confident age in which people write books about evangelism as if world evangelisation is going to be the ultimate triumph of human technology, we need to get back to the simplicity of this verse – that it was the Lord who added to their number.

Of course, he did it through the preaching of the apostles, through the witness of the ordinary church members, through their life of love. But *he* did it. Nobody else can do it. I think the major lesson we need to learn in evangelism is to humble ourselves before the sovereignty of our Lord Jesus Christ.

(ii) He 'added to the church those who were being saved'. These things went together. He did not add them to the church without saving them, and he did not save them without adding them to the church.

(iii) He did it daily. The Lord added to their number 'day by day'. We need to go back to that expectation. They did not regard evangelism as an occasional or sporadic activity. It was as continuous as their worship. I know churches that have not had a convert for ten years. They would not know what to do with one if they got one. We should be expecting the church to grow. We should be *expecting* the church to be continuously reaching out into the community for Christ.

These four marks of the renewed church apply to four relationships. *First* these Christians were related to the apostles, as we need to be across the centuries, to sit at the apostles' feet as they did in the New Testament. A renewed church is an apostolic church. *Secondly* they were related to each other. They loved each other. They cared for each other. They supported each other. *Thirdly* they were related to God. They worshipped God in the temple and in the home with joy and with reverence. They were a worshipping community. *Fourthly* they were related to the world outside. They were reaching out into the community.

Some years ago I visited one of the countries of Latin America, and I heard of a group of students who had visited every church in a certain city to try to find what they were looking for, and had been unable to find it so had dropped out. Naturally I pricked up my ears and asked, 'What were they looking for and unable to find?' You will be as astonished as I was that they went right through these four points without realising what they were doing. They were looking for biblical, contemporary preaching that relates the word of God to the contemporary world; for a living, loving fellowship; for worship in which we bow down to the living God; for a compassionate outreach into the community. Amazing, isn't it! The New Testament Church, and just what those young people were looking for today.

We don't need to wait for the Holy Spirit to come. The Holy Spirit did come, at Pentecost, and he has never left the Church. Indeed there is a sense in which Pentecost cannot be repeated, any more than Christmas, Good Friday, Easter or Ascension Day. Jesus was born once, died once, rose once, ascended once, and sent his Holy Spirit once. And he is still here, in the Church, which is his temple.

One thing more must be said. We need to acknowledge Christ's Lordship and his rightful possession. We need to submit to his sovereignty, his direction. Then our churches will become more like this church in Jerusalem in their biblical doctrine, loving fellowship, living worship, and ongoing, outgoing evangelism.

May God keep this vision before us.

Notes

Chapter 1: A medieval building for the 21st century or 'If I was going there, I wouldn't start from here'

1 A Sennockian is a native of Sevenoaks.

Chapter 2: This is Sevenoaks

1 Knole House was given to the National Trust in 1947 by the Sackville family, for whom it is still their home.

2 First published by the Caxton and Holmesdale Press in 1964 with several later impressions.

3 Connex Southeast Press Office.

4 There are six state primary schools in the town, each with good records: County Primary, Amherst, St John's, St Thomas's, Riverhead and Lady Boswell's. Then there are five private or prep schools: Sevenoaks Prep in nearby Godden Green, Solefields, Granville, Walthamstow Hall Junior and The New Beacon.

5 The Parochial Church Council (PCC) is the governing body of an Anglican parish church. It is elected by its members.

6 Phyllis Pearsall died in 1996. Her autobiography *A-Z Maps: the personal story - From bedsitter to household name* (Geographers' A-Z Map Company Ltd, 1990) traces A-Z's growth. With 250 titles, it has become one of the largest independent map publishing companies in the UK.

7 From *The Contemporary Christian* (IVP, 1992). See pp521ff of 1999 edition in *The Essential John Stott* (IVP).

Chapter 3: Problems and a solution

1 Anglican churches have two wardens, who are lay members of the congregation, and who work closely with the Rector on issues of policy and practice. They are, in effect, the senior members of the Parochial Church Council.

2 The story of the building project at All Souls was told by Mary Endersbee in *Hidden Miracles at All Souls* (Lakeland, 1977).

3 Robert Potter also designed the Millmead Centre in Guildford, re-ordered Christ Church, Woking, and oversaw the underpinning of St Stephen's, Walbrook, London.

Chapter 4: Looking at the options

1 See *The Times* 27 December 1996 and *The Daily Telegraph* 28 December 1996.

2 For the story of the Cambridge Seven, see J.C Pollock *The Cambridge Seven* (IVP, 1955; Marshall Pickering / OMF, 1985).

Chapter 5: Leading up to the big decision

1 To grant a Faculty is, in this sense, to give formal permission for the work to be carried out. It must have seemed ironic as time went on that the word comes from the Latin root meaning 'easy'!

2 The doctrine of the sufficiency of Scripture means simply that we don't need anything else alongside it as a guide and authority for living. There will always, of course, be a need for people and for books, videos, etc to help us understand it and apply it.

3 See Romans 5: 1-5

4 See 2 Corinthians 9:6ff. It is worth reading to the end of the chapter. As with every response we are invited to make to God in Scripture, it is in the context of what he has done for us.

5 St Nicholas Court, now on the site of the Parish Hall, was constructed by Tatham Homes.

6 The China Inland Mission is now OMF International with workers from 30 nations serving throughout East Asia.

Chapter 6: Two million pounds is a lot of money

1 Margaret Durdant-Hollamby tells the story in her autobiography *Life's not a rehearsal* (Durdant-Hollamby, 1998). She was made an MBE in honour of her achievement in 1994.

2 See Mark 12: 41-44.

Chapter 7: The exile

1 See Appendix 2 'How the undercroft was built' by Tony Cantrell for an explanation of 'piling'.

Chapter 8: Getting ready to move back 'home'

1 For several of the St Nicholas designs, see Angela Dewar *The New Church Kneeler Book* (Search Press, 1997).

Chapter 9: Building for the gospel

1 The UCCF Professional Groups provide a forum for this. For details contact the Professional Groups Secretary at UCCF, 38 de Montfort Street, Leicester LE1 7GP (email: email@uccf.org.uk). Christians at Work gives support to Christian fellowships in the workplace, and to individual Christians. For details contact the General Secretary, Christians at Work, 148 Railway Terrace, Rugby, CV21 3HN (email: caw@freeuk.com).

2 *Expository preaching in a postmodern world.* Cambridge papers 7:3. September 1998 (email: cpapers@campublic.co.uk).

3 See *Thank God it's Monday* (Scripture Union, 1994) by Mark Greene, Director of the Institute for Contemporary Christianity, for a helpful and readable look at this issue.

4 See Colossians 1:16,17.

5 For more information on such openings, contact the 9:38 Web, 301 Kingston Road, Wimbledon Chase, London SW20 8LB (email: admin@nine-38.u.net.com). The emphasis on all 9:38 placements is that of training for future ministry. This network takes its name from the Lord's invitation to pray for new workers (Matthew 9:38).

Chapter 11: For any churches that are wavering

1 See 1 Thessalonians 5:11; 2 Corinthians 13:10; 1 Corinthians 14:12,26. Taken from Mark Ashton's article *Why, where and how should Christians meet?* published in *Evangelicals Now*, February 1993. Copies are available from The Round at St Andrew the Great Church Office, Manor Street, Cambridge CB1 1LQ.

2 The Congregational Board is the elected group of representatives in Presbyterian churches to discuss matters of congregational concern.

3 Rather than creating synods, Presbyterian government groups congregations geographically into Presbyteries, where each church is represented by one minister and one lay elder. The Presbytery has ultimate legal, spiritual and financial jurisdiction in major congregational issues, including expenditure on buildings.

Appendix 1

'Now to him who is able'

This setting of Ephesians 3:20,21 was written by Peter Young for the re-opening of St Nicholas on 21 June 1995. He has kindly made it available for use in worship by any church.

Appendix 2

How the undercroft was built

Tony Cantrell, a member of St Nicholas and a consulting engineer with Cameron Taylor Bedford, explains what was actually happening over the 22 months of 'exile'.

St Nicholas Church was built in traditional materials. The present building was started in the 14th century, and has been added to at various times since. The internal columns are of stone construction, as are the external walls, which are 800mm (32 inches) thick. The weight of the building lies mostly in the stone structure, as the roof is of lightweight, timber construction. The building's foundation (or footings) are set at shallow depth in a deep stratum of sand.

Because of this shallowness, any support system introduced in the proposed scheme to form a basement must provide support at a shallow depth for the existing footings.

The foundations of the walls and the internal columns of the church need to be extended downwards to allow the basement rooms to be formed. This process is known as underpinning.

Walls are typically underpinned by digging out the ground below a short length of wall, down to the new required footing level, and then building a new wall and footing under the existing wall. Thus the foundation of the whole wall may be lowered in sections.

A similar process is not possible with a column, as it is too small an element (on plan) to underpin in sections. Because of this, a column has to be temporarily supported while the ground under it is removed and another foundation and column is built directly beneath the existing one.

At St Nicholas, this was achieved by installing 220mm (9 inch) diameter concrete piles in a group round each column, to a depth of 14.5 metres (about 48 feet) into the ground. A reinforced concrete collar was cast on top of these piles and around the column base, which effectively transferred the column load from the existing foundation onto the group of piles round each column.

The collars round the base of each column were then interconnected by a grillage of concrete tie beams, running both across the church and down the length of the nave. With the internal columns thus supported on piles, and with the whole system kept in place by the tie beams, the main excavation could take place round (and *under*) the stone columns in the church.

The foundations of the church walls were then underpinned as described earlier, and the reinforced concrete floor and walls to the new basement were constructed.

New internal columns were then built inside each pile group from the basement floor to the underside of the concrete collars round the foot of the existing stone columns.

With the internal columns now supported from basement level, the parts of the concrete piles from basement to ground level were redundant and were cut out and removed.

The grillage of concrete tie beams now formed a support system to the new concrete ground floor of the church, which was cast over these beams. This completed the construction of the new basement (or undercroft) under the existing medieval church.

We are grateful to the following people, and to all who worked with them, to achieve what was done:

Sarum Partnership *Architects*: Robert Potter OBE, Rex Butland, Tony Foster, Don Hargreaves. Interior design: Margaret Potter

Ove Arup *Structural engineers*: Poul Beckmann, Peter Lunoe

Wilson Colbeck *Quantity surveyor*: Janet Brown

Peter Jay and Partners *Lighting engineer:* Peter Jay, *Heating engineer*: Dennis Coomber

Public Address consultant: Don Feltham

Oxford Archaeological Unit *Director*: David Miles

James Longley *Director*: Richard Constable, *Contracts Manager:* Colin Baker, *Site Manager* Gary Harper, *Ganger*: Tim Chapman

Appendix 3

Sevenoaks timeline from 1120 to present

1120 Earliest reference to St Nicholas in the *Textus Roffensis* compiled under Bishop Ernulf. The town was then known as Seouenaca.

1217 Master Aaron instituted as first Rector of Sevenack.

1418 Sevenoaks School founded.

1533 John Frith, born in Westerham in 1503, and an old boy of Sevenoaks School, is burned at the stake on 4th July in Smithfield, London, for his part in the English Reformation. He had previously worked with William Tyndale in translating the Bible into English. To this day, a rose is placed on the pulpit of the parish church in Westerham on the Sunday nearest the anniversary of his death.

1570 Weekly Saturday market first set up.

1576 William Lambarde of Sevenoaks publishes *Perambulation of Kent*, the first county history of its kind.

1616 John Donne, later to be regarded as one of England's major metaphysical poets, appointed Rector of Sevenoaks by James I. He was Dean of St Paul's from 1573 and carried both titles until his death in 1631. It is not known whether he ever preached at St Nicholas, but it is likely he would have visited Knole to see the Duke of Dorset, one of his patrons.

1675 Lady Boswell leaves a bequest for the education of 12 poor scholars in the town. This is the beginning of what is to become Lady Boswell's School.

1734 First recorded cricket match on The Vine cricket ground.

1769 The Vine cricket ground set to have a place in the sport's history, as J Minshall scores the first ever century in the game, playing for the Duke of Dorset XI against Sevenoaks.

1774 John Wesley opens the Methodist Chapel in Redmans Place. Wesley was a friend of Vincent Perronet, vicar of Shoreham, and visited the town frequently until 1790, the year before his death.

1778 Jane Austen stays with her Uncle Francis at the Red House. It is widely held that both Hunsford and Rosings Park in *Pride and Prejudice* were influenced by her Sevenoaks memories.

1797 A benefactor gives £1,000 for an organ, which is placed in the gallery of the bell tower. Blocking out light from the large west window, it makes the church rather gloomy.

1814 Major work completed which left the original building considerably altered: outside walls are raised which reduce the slope of the roofs; battlements are added; the tower is strengthened; a new clock is installed; the ceiling of the nave is plastered and painted; clerestory windows are added. The cost is £10,000 covered by a special rate levied on all landowners. The debt is not finally cleared until 1870. With a town population of 2,279 (1801 census) Sevenoaks now has a church which can seat a quarter of them.

1818 The first school building for Lady Boswell's is opened on London Road

1862 A railway station is opened at Bat and Ball. A second line reaches Tubs Hill (Sevenoaks mainline station) in 1867. E M Nesbit's *The Railway Children*, though written in 1906 – many years after she left the area – is based on her memories of the embankment and tunnel at Knockholt.

1868 Hodder and Stoughton open premises at 27 Paternoster Row, London, with five titles on their list. They move to 40 Bedford Square in 1906. Their Dunton Green base closes in 1995. Both families came from Sevenoaks.

1889 The last journey of the London – Sevenoaks stage coach.

1902 Seven oak trees are planted on the side of the Vine Cricket Ground to mark the coronation of Edward VII.

H G Wells lives in Eardley Road, Sevenoaks while writing *The Time Machine*

1922 Winston Churchill buys Chartwell in Westerham for £5,000. He is to be Prime Minister from 1940-45 and 1951-55. He loves Chartwell where he escapes to paint and write. The house needs considerable repair when the Churchills move in, and a doctor recalls visiting a patient there who was sitting up in bed with an umbrella! Churchill's practical abilities are shown in the celebrated photograph, on display in the house, of his bricklaying, watched by his daughter.

1935 The north porch is added to the church, to commemorate the Jubilee of King George V.

1946 Seven oaks are planted near The Vine Tavern to commemorate the end of World War II.

1947 A fire in the roof of the nave. Timbers are replaced from the oak trees of Knole Park, as a gift from Lord Sackville. In the same year, Knole House is handed over to the National Trust by the Sackville family, and some of its supposed 365 rooms, 52 staircases, and 12 courtyards are opened to the public.

1954 Eric McLellan is installed as 49th Rector of St Nicholas. Over the course of his incumbency, serious thought is given to the buildings.

1955 The seven oak trees at the White Hart are dying. Lord Sackville presents seven new ones to the town, to replace them.

1966 The eight church bells are recast at the Whitechapel Foundry.

1970 Kenneth Prior is installed as 50th Rector. With the churchwardens and PCC, he is to make two major attempts at extensions between 1981 and 1983.

1972 Lady Boswell's moves to its present site on the edge of Knole Park.

1983 The Stag Theatre, founded through the efforts of Margaret Durdant-Hollamby, is opened in December.

1987 Miles Thomson is installed as 51st Rector. He is asked by the Trustees and the churchwardens to give urgent consideration to building needs. The famous hurricane on the night of 16 October uproots six of the seven oaks on the Vine Cricket Ground, and two of the oaks near the Vine Tavern.

1992 Sainsbury's opens a major store on the Otford Road. Out of town shopping has arrived despite protest from local traders and the Chamber of Commerce.

1993 Refurbishment of the Stag Theatre is finally completed, at a total cost of almost £3m.

1994 The last pile supporting new pillars is removed on 11 December. St Nicholas Church has had its ancient foundation entirely replaced.

1995 The new undercroft is formally returned on 19 June and crammed to capacity for a thanksgiving service on 21 June.

1998 The site of Marley Tiles head office in Dunton Green is now a giant Tesco store. Its arrival coincides with a major refurbishment for Sainsburys. Out of town shopping is established.

1999 The site near the station which houses the livestock market and the general market is sold to British Telecom for a major office complex. The livestock market, with its earliest beginnings in AD780, closes. The general market moves to the town centre.

St Nicholas hires the Stag Theatre for a series of presentations relating the first century gospel to some 21st century concerns: sport, ethics, ecology, pluralism, and family life – all under the title *Life 2000*. As the third millennium AD is about to open, members of St Nicholas take a short, first-century account of the life, death and resurrection of Jesus Christ, written by a doctor, to homes in the parish.

2000 The Stag Theatre is the venue for a further series of five evening events, for the people of Sevenoaks to look at the Christian faith for themselves.

For a more detailed chronicle of the history of the church, see David Killingray, *St Nicholas Parish Church, Sevenoaks, Kent: A brief history* (Boswell Books; first published 1990). ❧

The first bell is unloaded after all eight were recast at the Whitechapel Foundry, June 1966.
Photo by kindness of Alex Watson, Sevenoaks Chronicle